The Heron Spirals

A COMMONPLACE BOOK

Cover illustration and all internal artwork by Roderick MacIver, www.herondance.org
Design by Alison R. Hall, Design en Plus
Photo of author by Christina Guimond
Printed in Canada by Marquis

Library and Archives Canada Cataloguing in Publication

Parry, Caroline Balderston 1945-
The Heron Spirals: A Commonplace Book /Caroline Balderston Parry, art by Roderick MacIver
ISBN: 978-0-9919674-0-7

Cataloguing data available from Library and Archives Canada

Published by Britannia Arts
90 Britannia Road, Ottawa, Ontario, Canada K2B 5W5
514-622-2173
www.carolinebalderstonparry.com/site/The-Heron-Spirals

The Heron Spirals

A COMMONPLACE BOOK

Caroline Balderston Parry

Art by Roderick MacIver

BRITANNIA ARTS, OTTAWA

*Dedicated to Susan Pepper, who understood my heron connection,
and to any others for whom the little brown badger voices of despair seem too loud.
May you find renewal, clarity, and faith in Spirit and in your precious, resilient self.*

TABLE *of* CONTENTS

*I prefer the pleasure
of the journey through the spiral.*

Coming Home to Myself by Marion Woodman

How do we find common language for our spiritual journeys, each one so individual and unique? This collection of mid-life journal extracts, integrated with my reflections upon them, chronicles my inner and outer worlds during an approximately fifteen-year period. It is also about my surprising and inspiring heron encounters; the whole is meant to share my expanding spiritual life. I want the herons that I find so transformative to be a feathered link between you, as my precious readers, and myself, want the herons to provide a bridge between my story and your own spiritual explorations.

My life cycle journey, beginning in Pennsylvania and Massachusetts, moved through childhood and young adulthood to marriage, parenthood and early widowhood. My outward travels evolved to include sojourns in India, England, Israel and a recent two years in Ohio, while coming to call Canada my home. I have traversed changing career roles and new lovers, and roamed through varied stages: my spirit has grown with each change, in each place. Revisiting many of life's lessons from different vantage points, my path has wound through the years in more of a spiral than a straight progression.

I view these spiraling experiences through the lens of being a member of the Society of Friends, or Quakers. Born into a large established Quaker family, I attended a Quaker high school and raised my children in the Society, maintaining an active role in whatever local Friends Meeting of which I have been a part. This lifelong spiritual identity and practice for me began within Christianity and now embraces the world's religious diversity. During the 1990s I discovered I am also a person who finds a sense of communion with herons; in the last decade my spirituality has had an additional Unitarian Universalist slant due to my salaried work.

As a Quaker I sit in silent, open waiting, in community with others and with what today I call the Great Spirit of many names. Occasionally in our Meeting for Worship, in response to some power greater than myself, I speak a message that fills my awareness.

On other occasions I may sing, or weep copiously. In still other places or times of worship I laugh or dance; often I feel at one with Spirit and the group; sometimes awestruck or transformed.

At many different times and places I have written down my thoughts in journals and letters, occasionally as poetry or as dialogue with Spirit. I've also listened to — and hungrily read — the words of a myriad other seekers, trying to hear the voice of "love and mystery that some call God." Sometimes that voice has "spoken" through deep conversation with, or even casual comments from, friends and relations, and during my heron years, through those striking birds. Perhaps you, too, have moved among similar life dimensions. I wonder who — or what — have been your companions?

Along my way I have discovered that although this path I walk is precisely mine, it overlaps with innumerable others. And so I have collected parallel quotes from a variety of other people's inward and outward travels, as well as related poems, prayers and songs. These amplify my heron experiences, and Rod MacIver's lovely heron artwork illustrates aspects of the shared road.

What has emerged is a collection resembling the old commonplace books. Since the 15th century, and the increasing availability of paper for writing, "commonplaces" have been a kind of themed personal scrapbook, filled with writing of interest to each book's creator. Commonplaces are best known in England; the protagonist in *The English Patient* used his copy of Herodotus as a commonplace book, and W. H. Auden wrote *A Certain World: A Commonplace Book*, in 1970 as a kind of autobiography. In Lemony Snicket's *A Series of Unfortunate Events* a number of characters keep commonplace books. In this age of the internet, some writers have drawn analogies between web blogs and commonplaces; sites like Pinterest, which provide both visual and verbal collections of what intrigues the creators, might be electronic commonplaces. Whatever you label it, welcome to this journal-keeper's musings on herons, on Spirit and on a rich and complex life, complemented by the work of so many others.

I hope this little book will touch both those who have found a faith community or spiritual practice that suits them, and those who have not. I especially hope my writing will reach those who love the natural world and its herons as I do! The sense of the profound we find in nature is universal, shared with anyone who seeks a deeper understanding of life. Furthermore, I invite you to respond to this volume as if it were your own commonplace book, adding to it as you see fit, or making comments via my website: www.carolinebalderstonparry.com/site/The-Heron-Spirals.

May the words and images I have chosen to chart my course here resonate for you, wherever you may be on your own journey. May these meditations on the herons, and on other aspects of creation that reflect my own world, help you find renewal, clarity, strength and meaning in yours.

THE SOURCES OF THE SPIRALS

My heron account is faceted by a quantity of outward turbulence: the story includes how I and my English-American-Canadian family moved to Ottawa in the midst of adult career shifts, marital struggles and teenage school issues, and how my life has subsequently evolved. There is a parallel, quieter narrative, as well, a spiralling thread that chronicles my inner life.

In 1994, I began to document and reflect on my life as it unfolded following the ideas of Julia Cameron in *The Artist's Way*. She recommends daily "morning pages," or stream-of-consciousness writing, and I often pour out those entries still, collecting them in looseleaf binders. I also write periodically in another smaller journal of the bound book variety, to remember significant insights, and I keep a bedtime desk diary of daily exercise, prayers and gratitude. All three of these forms might record a heron encounter; all three nourish me and have been resources for this book.

Throughout *The Heron Spirals*, some of my journal entries are dated, while others are composites, crafted from several predecessors. My reflections are interwoven in a contrasting font. The whole series cannot always be arranged chronologically, because as we discover by living it, life is seldom linear. I use the word "spiral" because I find we circle around and revisit many life questions — such as how to trust rather than fear the unknown — from new points in time or physical location. For this commonplace book, I have crafted logical, lyrical sequences, winding inward.

Quotations are given with the author's name and book title, where known; for some fuller source data, see Credits and Notes on page 174.

Time itself is cyclic, and by the spiral of its
returning seasons we review the progress and growth
of our own understanding. Ours is the spiral house
we build to keep us from life's continuous outpouring,
from an otherwise unchecked flow into the unknown.

The Mystic Spiral, Journey of the Soul BY JILL PURCE

ACKNOWLEDGEMENTS

This book grew through years of gestation, many of them challenging, and there are undoubtedly people whose names I cannot now remember but who helped to birth these pages. However, I am hugely grateful to my re-discovered high school English teacher, Chuck Kruger, and my Unitarian Church of Montreal colleague, Sandra Hunt, for significant editorial help.

Further warm thanks are due to the following known readers and supporters, in alphabetical order:

Sarah Albu, Alan and Virginia Allport, Betsy Balderston, Elaine Bishop, Joan Broadfield, Valerie Brown, Sandy Byer, Elizabeth Cave, Rose Marie Cipryk, Alice Dawson, Roger Diggle, Mary Lib Eyerer, Mike Feuerstack, Andrew Francis, Kathy Gallagher, Carlene Gardner, Cara Graver, Camilla Gryski, O. John Hawkins, Joan Horn, Jesse Husk, Cricket Keating, Jane Keeler, Angela Klassen, Bill and Laura Laky, Christina MacEwan, Rhondda MacKay, Carole Martignacco, Liz Mathieson, Lanie Melamed, Tanya Middlebro, Ramona Christine Hayes Moon, Evalyn Parry, Richard Reed Parry, Anne Balderston Peery, Susan Pepper, Susan Robertson, Suzanne Robertson, Shirley Russ, Bridgid Schorer, Peni Schwartz, Ruth Shilling, Julie Sullivan, Susan Tanner, Jane Waterston, Marian Wyse, and those un-recalled but also influential contributors! Finally, I thank and glory in my splendid designer, Alison Hall.

My path curves onward, with the herons as my guide. At last this commonplace book will share my special heron moments: enjoy, drink deeply, rise, soar!

Before

Great Blue Heron

Tall solemn bird
wades in the water,
wary and wise; slow to startle
or to rise ...
Now great wings open wide,
pushing off, pulsing high –
long legs lifting, head leading
above the calm lake surface.
Then – sudden, surprising! –
rising to greet the real heron I see
the clear reflection of itself:
shimmering wings respond to wings widespread;
watery body below grey, feathered breast
in moving, mirrored, harmony.
Oh Great Spirit, so buoy me
that I, too, will spread my wings and try
to fly this fearlessly,
knowing that my silent cries
and surge of soul – like heron rise –
shall answered be.

Mud Lake, Ottawa

. . . .

15th August 1990

Yesterday on my run ... I saw two great blue herons: it felt like an omen!

27th August 1993

... A heron rose up from near the point where my grandfather tree stands, so I could really see the reflection that's so important in my poem — reminding me I will be buoyed by the Great Spirit, I am....

Mid-November 1993 (scrap paper log)

Over approximately two months, I have had 33 days when I saw at least one heron! What a wide blessing....

> We use imagery to translate the immense unknowable Sacred
> into symbolic terms we can relate to. We pray to a "Thou", not an "it."
> We have "peopled" the heavens with angels and attributed
> the earth and sky with familial ties:
> Brother Sun, Sister Moon, Mother Earth. We look for ways
> to be in relationship with the energy of the universe.
>
> *Life's Companion* by Christina Baldwin

I have carried a sense of herons as sacred in my heart for many years. Maybe this heron attunement began in 1990 with our little dog, Jessie, whom we adopted when we moved from downtown Toronto to the west end of Ottawa, a then family of four. We were myself, American born, my English husband and our two Canadian offspring. Our daughter was finishing high school, our son in middle school. He had been longing for a dog of his own, in true youngster fashion, and we had promised that when we resettled in the area known as Britannia-on-the-Bay, and had lots of access to nature, we'd find him a furry companion. Jessie came to live with us just after we moved into our new house, with its big fenced garden. We not only had space for her to dash about, but our property backed onto the Britannia Conservation Area, with new acres of woods, field and swampland to explore, as well as access to the Ottawa River.

I started taking Jessie on my morning jogs, and wrote in my occasionally-kept journal about my first encounter with herons in Mud Lake, the centre of the conservation area. I began to craft my heron poem soon after that sighting, but didn't finish it until April 1993. Later that year a close friend called the herons my "power birds"; I remember that I did recognize that truth, yet found her language embarrassing.

My heron poem was published in *Friends Journal*, a major Quaker monthly, in February 1995. Even though I had noted how that heron rising might presage great meaning, almost five years earlier; even though I had wondered about totems or special guidance associated with certain life forms during those intervening years, I was hesitant to fully accept my own heron connection. Seeing my poem in print validated that reality for my doubting self.

A decade later I heard an uplifting Unitarian Universalist sermon in which the minister referred to Mary Jo Leddy's proposal that, rather than the familiar little white dove, a better, more Canadian image of the Holy Spirit would be a great blue heron. I was transfixed! Herons as symbols of the Holy Spirit had become truths of my own experience. In fact many Native peoples have long held the great blue heron sacred; evidently
I am not alone.

Among traditional Native Americans and other tribal peoples,
totems are the enduring animal symbols that allow people
to explore the mysteries of life and the spirit world....
Each animal embodies certain strengths and attributes
that the spiritual seeker can embrace and follow
on the path of self-exploration.

Totems, The Transformative Power of Your Personal Animal Totem
BY BRAD STEIGER

Skimming the waters
skipping, swooping through clear air,
swallows: wild, wide, sweet.

. . . .

August, early 1990s

Plop! As I arrive at the muddy water's edge, a frog plunges through the duckweed at my feet. A little farther away, a family of wood ducks half-scamper over the water, half-fly off in fright at my appearance. Swallows swirl above them. The breeze ruffles my hair and sways the purple loosestrife growing tall beside me. Looking for herons, as I usually do, I scan the far green shore line, examine two old beaver lodges where herons often stand, and glory in the white cupped beauty of the water lilies scattered across the lake surface.

> *The bird generally represents your higher self or wisdom nature.*
> *The other animals represent your creative and sexual energy.*
> *Studying them both can give you clues about your nature.*
> *It can increase self-awareness and self-acceptance.*
>
> *Sacred Living, A Daily Guide* BY ROBIN HEREENS LYSNE

How hesitant I was in naming this significant relationship or acknowledging my openness to heron "messengers!" But just how <u>did</u> I come to be standing there, as I did and do so many mornings, surveying the rippling waters and complex natural life of that swampy lake? How is it that Mud Lake, part of a wetlands conservation area bordering the water purification system of the City of Ottawa, on the south side of the broad Ottawa River, hemmed in on the non-river side by distant apartment buildings, came to be a wilderness refuge and place of daily spiritual renewal for me? And just what "Way opened," as Quakers phrase it, to put me on that shore so regularly? When I study the lake, I survey my past mid-life years, watching for herons, noting the mileposts.

Slowly, not always surely, I have come to accept and declare that great blue herons are a precious part of my spiritual life. To me, these large, long-legged birds are grace-full, not at all ungainly; their appearance portentous. My encounters with herons — or even with just a consciousness of herons — repeatedly help me find Spirit, my Divine centre.

We embark on our spiritual journeys in order to make sense of our lives.

Sacred Circles: A Guide To Creating Your Own Women's Spirituality Group
BY ROBIN DEENS CARNES AND SALLY CRAIG

*Reflecting pool –
blue heron balances
on itself.*

BY PAMELA MILLER

. . . .

1990s, no specific date

On my run today I end up at my lookout point in the conservation area, and spot a sentinel heron about halfway across the lake. I have binoculars with me, so observe him closely for a bit, as he waits — for what? — quite motionless. Then I stand still myself, asking for help to quiet my internal dialogue, my rushing mind with its lists of all there is to do. As I watch this erect grey-blue shape, being here, now, fully myself, means a total immersion in knowing that all is well. Centuries ago Saint Julian of Norwich, the anchorite, affirmed that "All shall be well, and all shall be well, and all shall be well again." Today I get to be relaxedly of faith that my life is unfolding as it should. I salute that heron, nod towards yet another one fishing farther across the water, and turn toward home, holding heron stillness within my heart.

> *For it is only framed in space that beauty blooms.... Here on this*
> *island I have had space.... Here there is time; time to be quiet; time*
> *to work without pressure; time to think; time to watch the heron,*
> *watching with frozen patience for his prey.... Then communication*
> *becomes communion and one is nourished as one never is by words.*
>
> *Gift From the Sea* BY ANNE MORROW LINDBERGH

In recent years herons have helped me learn to start the day-by-day business of moving forward from a core place of Spirit. Over and over I have seen them, standing still in a lake or river, or along the margin of a swamp or pond, reminding me in some mysterious way to "Be still and know...."

What does it mean to be still, then? For a heron I imagine it means merging into a timeless *now*, fully present in each moment, aware of water, fish, lily pads, wind. Herons seem so good at this, not moving for long stretches of time, then simply cocking an angular head, or taking a few steps, spreading out a wing and folding it back inward again, turning to face another direction, and returning to watchful stillness. How often this is hard for me! How deeply I am challenged to be still. And yet, what a heart-lifting messenger!

In Greece the heron was sacred to Athene and Aphrodite,

carrying their messages to humans....

Ancient Egyptians associated the heron with the rising sun

and the return of the resurrected god Osiris.

It signified regeneration of life.

Animal Magick BY D. J. CONWAY

Herons are also full of import for me when I see them flying. Early on in this midlife period of my heron years, my clay-working, sculpture-making friend Chris gave me a beautiful little clay bas-relief of a heron flying. How pleased I was by her gift, a still rendition of movement! I felt even more delighted when I found the perfect place in our front hall to hang her heron plaque, its faint blue-on-pale-yellow colours picked up by the deeper yellow of the painted wall and the golden brown wood of the stairway around it.

I installed that first piece of heron art with a sense of its auspicious placement, there in the transition space of the front entry way, watching over me in my incessant to-and-fro life. In fact, I sometimes pass that little clay heron with its blue-grey wings outspread, and ask for help with whatever task is at hand, whatever journey. This quality of invocation must be similar to what faithful Jews feel about their small prayer container, the *mezuzah*, installed on the front door post of their homes. Or perhaps it is related to the Hindu practice of praying to Ganesha, the guardian god, asking him for access to their major deities. How many different ways we humans have found to try and access the mysterious Divine.

My bas-relief heron in flight does seem to bless my home, reminding me of the wings of Spirit. I believe those vaster wings are always wafting over us, around me, and that whenever I remember that level of reality, remember that I am part of Spirit, my daily journey is less of a struggle. When I do affirm the spiritual dimension of my everyday existence, my life goes more smoothly, indeed, does its own soaring from a still centre.

Peace upon those who enter in;
Godspeed to those who depart;
Blessing upon those who dwell here.

BLESSING FROM THE LATIN

. . . .

21st August 1992

What a week of connections! I'm gradually beginning to feel back to normal after being away ten days, though I feel like the dog who has to turn round three times before she settles down.... On my third day at home I saw the heron twice, the first time flying and croaking at me, the second time standing: "Be still and know that I am God."

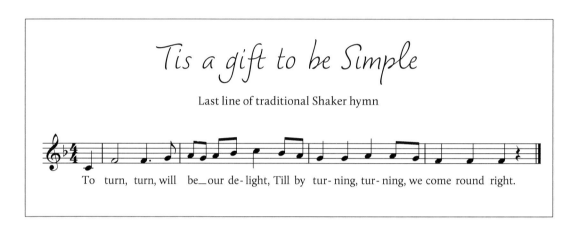

'Tis a gift to be Simple

Last line of traditional Shaker hymn

To turn, turn, will be—our de-light, Till by tur-ning, tur-ning, we come round right.

8th September 1993

... This afternoon I felt drawn down the straight path through the field and the woods. When I stepped up to an opening onto Mud Lake, off flew one heron and there was another, standing motionless and alert. I stood quietly watching them, feeling alert to Spirit myself, almost directly connected to some great Mystery through the herons.

> *My life has a swing to it, but also an unending surprise — it's not a circle but a spiral that I feel. And why shouldn't I feel a spiral, which is the natural pattern of growth and motion on a spinning planet? Winds move in spirals, ocean currents travel in spirals, sunflower seeds grow in spirals, our galaxy itself is a spiral. Why should my life be any different?*
>
> *Spirals, A Woman's Journey through Family Life* BY JOAN GOULD

L ooking for my records of heron encounters, I leaf through various journals and unearth files of long-ago letters. Truly the Chinese saying is right: "The palest ink is clearer than the sharpest memory."

Perhaps our recorded words are so helpful because they reveal how our inner life seems to be a process of spiral movement. Our bodies may grow taller, or older, and our lives may follow linear calendars, outwardly. But inwardly, we don't so much move straight through our issues as much as we seem to spiral around our hard learning places, circling through the cycle of the years, and frequently re-engaging with our own struggles. Sometimes we see from a new vantage point, and every so often we can tell we have made some headway, gained some wisdom.

Yet I often forget I have been *here* before, and old jottings may remind me. Recently I read over a page of conference notes from the 1980s and found I had had a remarkable encounter with the literal exhortation to "be still and know…." This was long before I had come to think of herons as teachers or messengers for myself. During that conference I had gone jogging in the woods alone, and I came upon an odd but beautiful gateway. Mysteriously parallel to the dirt road, a simple wooden arch between two posts led to nowhere in particular. On it was inscribed "Be still and know that I am God." (Psalms 46:10)

Frequently, when I read over old notes, I am surprised to see that rather than gaining a brand new awareness or grappling with what I thought was a fresh problem in the present, I have re-met an old insight or concern at a new level. Sometimes I rage at my slowness and boil with impatience at my need to relearn. It's better to be pleased to notice we have emerged at a different point on our spirals. If only incrementally, we have increased our understanding, improved skills, or gained experience. As I thumb through my volumes of self-writing, I realize that they are a kind of road map, giving evidence of my journey, labyrinthine though it may be.

A leading is more than Divine guidance…. Leadings exist in a context of
assumptions and of traditions. Part of understanding leadings is accepting as
a reality that God can and does say to us, "I want you to do this."
…Part of what makes us [Quakers] a unique people [is] the belief that God can
and will say that to us … and lead us, not into evil, but into goodness and unity.

From a talk given by Bill Kriedler at Friends General Conference Gathering 1997

14th September 1992

On the road home from the touching Quaker wedding of two elderly friends. Amazing! They were wartime sweethearts, lost track of each other, married other partners, and are now reunited after so many years apart! A beautiful, hot, end-of-summer day, and we stopped at the Black River, dark yet sparkling in the sunlight, its margins golden and purple with September flowers. I sensed we might see a heron, and just as we turned back towards the car, up one flew from the reeds quite near us! He spread his wings and called out hoarsely as he rose across the blue-black water and the autumn-coloured trees. He flew on, way down the river, steadily pumping those wonderful blue-grey wings. Another "Quoo-ooon-nnk" echoed across the distance.

I wait beside the flowing black water.
Only river's deep movement there,
and the clear air around filled with the wild cries of geese,
their feathered bodies instinctively winging on, above the trees
a rhythmic, changing wedge:

honk, flap, high calling. Listen!

Excerpt from my poem *May We Have Safe Passage*

Looking back, I reflect on that heron's loud sound, perhaps calling to me! I wonder about the phrases "being called" or "to have a calling". Quakers try to discern what is the best, Spirit-centred thing to do, to find "Way opening," or to have patient faith that "Way will open." It is a matter of listening to an internal voice, which for many people is a very "still small voice". Although some do feel they have received an important message or felt a strong leading, it's astonishing that Way seemed to open for the two who have just been married after all these years of disconnection! Would they say they were called, I wonder? Certainly they were miraculously led back to one another.

As for myself, I can find it excruciatingly difficult to listen inwardly, to discern the right way forward, whether the decision is a major one or just part of daily living. I often agonize over what step to take, and on a deeper level, over whether I am being called or led. Sometimes my path seems to receive a benison, some external sign that I have done or am doing the right thing. Perhaps this loving, late marriage which I was privileged to witness, and then the heron's strong-winged traveling, symbolize for me my own long journey. His "quo-onk" was an encouraging call, an echo of the poet Mary Oliver's wild geese, calling over and over to announce our "place in the family of things."

Calls are essential questions ... to which you need to respond, expose
yourself and kneel before ... you want a question that will become a
chariot to carry you across the breadth of your life, that will offer you
a lifetime of pondering, that will lead you towards what you need for
your integrity, draw you to what you need for your journey.

Callings: Finding and Following an Authentic Life BY GREG LEVOY

∙ ∙

26th August 1993

Third journal entry in one day.... Life is so confusing, I can't make sense of it all today! It's an August night at bedtime and I have had such a full day, crowned by doing a tai chi set on Britannia beach and hearing a pair of herons croak their greeting overhead....

The next morning: I'm rushing to be at my desk, but I want to pause first and affirm the herons in my life.... So many different sightings lately, and now twice on the beach a pair have seemed to call to me, croaking as they flew over Britannia Bay at dusk. I feel happily blessed to have these beautiful big birds as messengers or guides.

∙ ∙

31st August 1993

Late August morning, on a cottage dock on the Madawaska River: a hazy day, no heron (yet!) and windy. David and I are here for a little time together, talking about how thorny our relationship seems, about our counsellor's role, and our mutual sense of where we are now. When we arrived I saw a still heron in the bay nearby (called "Mud Bay," echoing our own "Mud Lake"), standing so long that I stood too, and prayed. That afternoon one was fishing mid-river in the marsh grass, pretty close and visible as we paddled by in the canoe, both going up and coming back down the river.

Yesterday we sat together on the dock and another heron waded right along this stretch of beach, HIS beach, I'd have said. He (or "she" — who knows? Their relative size is the only obvious gender difference) was fishing for some supper, hiding himself in the green and grey lines of the shore. I went out once more in the canoe, ostensibly to see the sunset, but watching for the heron, too. The rising moon was even more spectacular than the fading sun's pink glow over the dark mass of the shoreline trees.

It feels as if these herons, all busy about their business, are conveying a message to me about "carry on, keep working, you're doing well," each time I see them. How I hope that this will be so, despite the tangles of the many years of our marriage.... How I long to feel less distant from David, more wanted and treasured.

Today, when I went for my run to Mud Bay, where our friends say the heron lives, there one was, head alert in the long grass, neck almost a stem itself. I stood, too, affirming "Be still...," quieting my thoughts. Then she lifted up those strong proud wings and circled right around the entire bay area, quonking. I had a deeply satisfying long watch as she flew, promising her, "All right, heron, I'll carry on!", soaking up her shape and sound and silhouette: a true inspiration before we left for home.

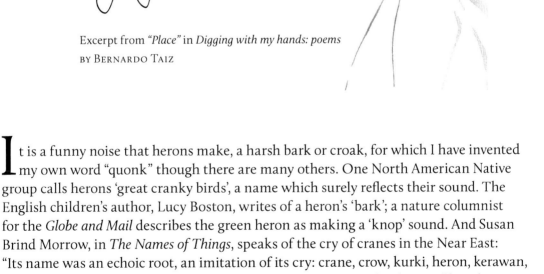

I try to imagine prayer like that, listening so intently in the early light and saying so little.

Excerpt from *"Place"* in *Digging with my hands: poems* by Bernardo Taiz

It is a funny noise that herons make, a harsh bark or croak, for which I have invented my own word "quonk" though there are many others. One North American Native group calls herons 'great cranky birds', a name which surely reflects their sound. The English children's author, Lucy Boston, writes of a heron's 'bark'; a nature columnist for the *Globe and Mail* describes the green heron as making a 'knop' sound. And Susan Brind Morrow, in *The Names of Things*, speaks of the cry of cranes in the Near East: "Its name was an echoic root, an imitation of its cry: crane, crow, kurki, heron, kerawan, geranos." My old English teacher, now living and writing in Ireland, gives "frarnk, frarnk" for his grey heron's croak, but cautions that it's "as unlike song as undertow."

Where religion requires a broad jump into the arms of authority,
the spiritual quest requires only a short step over the void. Its basic
assumption is: my life is the text within which I must find the
revelation of the sacred.

Hymns to an Unknown God BY SAM KEEN

After some fifteen years which began wonderfully and seemed well-balanced, our marriage became a constant struggle. Many couples have these mid-life crises about careers and children and whose needs come first. Neither of us could understand why it was so hard to reclaim the overwhelming love for one another we had begun with. We both wanted recognition in our work worlds, as well as at home; both felt each other was not as supportive of our roles and achievements as we craved. We also both longed to be the best parents we could be for our children, and that seemed to mean staying together. So, we hung in with each other and our difficulties over a period of about ten more years, through two sabbatical trips across the Atlantic and our major move to Ottawa.

Although I had fiercely resisted one more life change, it was in Ottawa that I began understanding herons as part of my spiritual life. A move that felt traumatic in the short term seems to have been transformative in the long term. Yet, what a challenge it has been for me to hold the bigger perspective! I love the words of a 17th century Quaker who spoke of feeling "wound into Largeness"; how often I long to let go of my smallness, to stop being so petty with someone — for sure with David during our married life — and to experience that Great Largeness in myself.

. . . .

Labour Day Saturday, 4th September 1993

We are in Montreal to help our daughter get settled for her second year of university. I imagine there's little chance of herons flying across the city treetops here today. But this has been my biggest heron week ever! Monday and Tuesday up at our friends' cottage (and along their Mud Bay) were heron-laden, then Wednesday morning at home again I ran and met a heron in our Mud Lake who quonked companionably to me. Thursday morning I didn't see one when I ran at home, but there were <u>loads</u> of heron moments that afternoon, when I stole an hour to go out with a new friend canoeing for the first time ever on Mud Lake. Finally, yesterday while walking dogs with my Ottawa friend Chris, we saw a heron fairly close to our path. It flew up and away across Mud Lake, broad-winged — we both were delighted!

When my new canoeing buddy arrived on Thursday, I thought how strange it was that I had not been out before on that lake in the summertime — though I ski and skate over it so often in winter. Mud Lake — despite its name — is far cleaner than I had imagined, and we had a wonderful sense of adventure as we paddled.

As for the herons, we followed one fellow for ages: initially he flew up from standing mid-lake, and perched high in the top of a big white pine; then, a dead elm. Eventually he floated down and across to the beaver lodge, and as he flexed his outstretched wings, up rose a slow second heron! Then as we canoed nearer to the beaver lodge, I pulled a huge grey feather from the water. It felt like a gift, and my companion encouraged me to think indeed it was. We talked about birds-as-messengers, and I just enjoyed being out on the lake, extending our friendship, feeling invigorated by those great grey-blue birds and their encompassing wing spans.

Coincidentally, here in Montreal, I have been talking with another old friend, Lanie, a woman in her 60s whose life and words give me courage, even as seeing herons seems to. She insists I take pride in how seasoned I myself am and how much work experience I do have, especially at moments when I think I am not prepared enough, or am self-critical of my considerable ability to — yes! — wing something. Clearly I must rise above the negative self-doubts, rise like the heron. I am keeping that feather I found, as a talisman and a reminder, in my journal.

They told the crane that
"These are the songs that we want to use,
   we want to use in our ceremonies."...

The crane informed 'em that
   "If you use my songs," he said,
   "I want you also to use my feathers."...

The white
the white feathers represent
peace
peace to people...
being dedicated and
pureness....

According to that story they don't belong to us
they belong to the crane,
We're just
on loan,
for those songs
and the feathers also....

Excerpts from the traditional origin story of the Yuchi people, quoted in *Folklife Center News* (see notes).

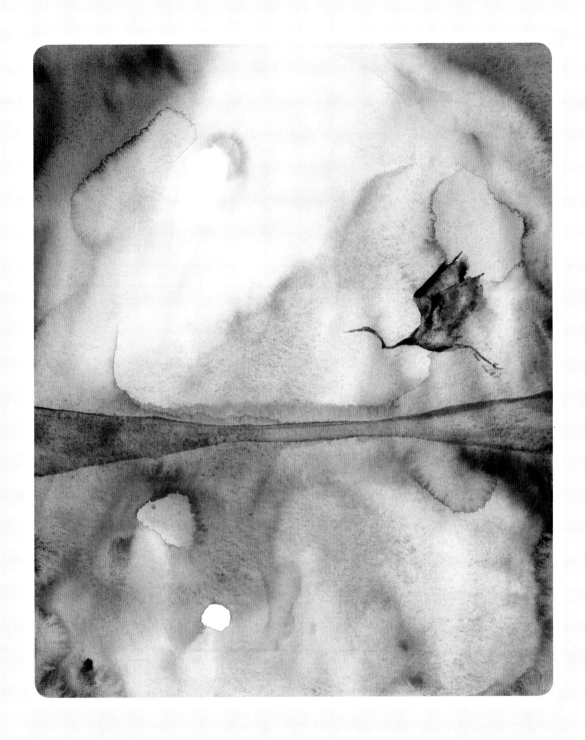

During that late summer period when our marriage was such a concern, I kept pushing myself to find the time and the wisdom to proceed with a publishing deadline, to stay centred, finish each task, and do them well. Though I often felt muddled and downhearted, I always ran in the morning before getting to work. I would find herons awaiting me, standing motionless and silent, or flapping slow, confident wings! Again and again, I was amazed by the herons' frequent appearances and found a sense of being supported and guided. Repeatedly, I came home from my exercise time encouraged by the herons' strong-winged abundance and by a feeling of synchronicity.

> ... a sheer earthly, deep earthly, sacred earthly consciousness:
> that what we see here and now is to bring us into a wider
> — indeed the very widest — dimension.

> Excerpt from *"Impermanence,"* BY RAINER MARIA RILKE
> in a 1925 letter to Witold Hulewicz, from the book *A Year With Rilke,*
> translated and edited by Joanna Macy and Anita Barrows

Reflecting on this period, I believe that committing myself to do ANY regular, aware practice, especially in the mornings, was and is important. By 1994, I had begun writing daily morning pages for self-care, and that process definitely evolved into a spiritual practice, a way to tune into both myself and the larger meanings around me. Some might think daily exercise has no spiritual relevance or meaning, but my experience says otherwise. My jogging was an additional way to get in positive gear for the day. Undertaken partly because it helped my body feel alive, and partly to take our dog Jessie out, my run literally forced me to go outside and look around.

Once outdoors, feeling the weather and the path I chose for my feet, I would become more conscious of my context, of coloured leaves or dropped feathers, of wind in my face, honking geese or the patient herons. How it all shifted my point of view! And is that not significant, to learn to put one's attention in the present moment of stone-in-the-path or bird-fluttering-nearby? Does it not increase our ability to be of courage, to be glad and confident?

In a later examination of these original journal entries, I discovered that there was more significance in my journal entry for that Labour Day in Montreal than I had noticed before. My earlier reflections failed to convey — perhaps I didn't truly understand — the full import of Lanie's words about "winging it," and a vital suggestion from her only made sense years later....

. . . .

4th September 1993

... She said my feeling bad-because-I'm-winging-something when I go to lead a workshop or etc is to be dropped — WINGING IT means I KNOW HOW TO DO IT and don't need all that preparation. In fact, from now on, I'll think of HERON WINGS and my new feather.

Further, Lanie thinks there is a book waiting to be written about how long it takes to heal and about how women have or have not solved mid-life relationship crises or dilemmas, and found (or not) late life companions/partners. She thinks I could do this — ??

I am somewhat staggered to see the idea of this book here, reading it over so much later. Obviously the thought had an impact, because my question marks reveal some inner response. If this IS that book, it certainly has taken a long time to birth! Meantime, Lanie herself birthed a group to fight breast cancer, and a wonderful community gathered around her in support, but she lost her life in the summer of 2004. I acknowledge her valiant spirit, and am grateful for her earlier encouragement. I still have that heron feather as well to remind me of my own wings.

> ... *Search for any metaphor whatsoever which will take you*
> *across the worldly divide whenever you need to be transported or*
> *comforted.... it's the history of [hu]mankind's search for holiness....*
> *You take whatever works from wherever you can find it, and you*
> *keep moving towards the light.*
>
> *Eat, Pray, Love: One Woman's Search for Everything Across*
> *Italy, India and Indonesia* BY ELIZABETH GILBERT

• •

6th September 1993

Monday night, Labour Day itself: We're home again, and I'm trying out what it feels like to sleep alone in our daughter's room, in part because I've been contemplating it for ages, and partly because David is having severe back problems and I wanted both of us to be less disturbed. Plus I long for this temporary separation to reveal a renewed commitment to one another.... Is this a critical moment? Is this related to all the herons? A Quaker friend says herons are to do with my sacred dreams....

• •

To love thee strongly,
To honour thee deeply,
To grow with thee carefully,
To cleave unto thee gently,
I plight my troth.

With this ring I thee wed,
With my body I thee worship,
And with all my worldly goods I thee endow.

From our Quaker marriage vows written in India, 1968

• •

12th September 1993

Mid-September and I'm seeing herons almost daily! Walking our dogs yesterday, dear Chris and I saw three, flying wonderfully close above us at the river's edge. I feel I really must start to list their occurrence, must look at the fullness of the herons in my life these days.... Going to go run now, thinking about their meaning, hoping to see more of them! (Is this a turning point in my healing?) The herons' frequency amazes me! It's as if I have been in some sort of spiritual drought and now have been drinking in so many herons, meeting them almost every day, up at Mud Bay, here in Mud Lake....

. . . .

29th September 1993

Money!! Bounced cheques right and left! It feels like this problem of not enough money, not enough shared planning with David, is even worse this fall than last....

12th October 1993

Another book deadline met, hurrah! Yesterday two herons blessedly near, strong flying across Mud Lake.

30th October 1993

I suspect the herons really have flown south for the season now. The last one I saw was a small bittern-type heron about two months after the beginning of this blessed-abundance-of-herons. My Toronto friend Sandy says they are my "power animals" — they are, though I still feel awkward in naming them as such. Nonetheless, how sustained I have felt by these herons and by their seeming constancy. I have been so aware of, and grateful for, the support I sense every time I see them.

. . . .

There were always birds around us. The tall goliath heron and the fish eagle
were our companions all the way. They flew — tense and slow
on their giant wings — alongside the boat....

The Names of Things by Susan Brind-Morrow

During that fall of 1993 I was pushing hard to finish my non-fiction young people's book, *Eleanora's Diary*. I was also committed to working as an "artist in residence" at a local school for a month, and then went on the road to promote the book. At home, I mourned the absence of my daughter, spreading her own wings, and fretted about our marriage. David and I were both tense about money issues, as we tried to finance our daughter's university life and find ways for me to earn more. Still, I managed to get out for my run with Jessie every morning before setting off to school. My journal entries were rushed, though often exultant about heron encounters.

Moments or things or people that empower us can be so happenstance — a chance verse of a song, a line in a book, a talk or a walk that is opportune. Since the early '90s, when the mysterious winged grace of these herons began to "happen" in my life, herons have become my almost regular though unbidden companions. Rather than try to explain their appearance, I simply acknowledge they give me a spiritual lift, and I give thanks, thanks even to the Great Heron Spirit.

All waders have similar physical characteristics — long, thin legs, long necks, and sharp bills. These physical characteristics are important to understand.... Legs enable animals and people to move about on the earth. They are symbols of balance, and they represent an ability to progress and evolve. Also, the longer the legs, the deeper the water the heron will feed in. The deeper life can be explored.... When it feeds, it stands in the water, reflecting a connection to the earth, while implying the exploration of other dimensions on the earth (water element). It is important for anyone with a heron totem to explore various activities and dimensions of earth life.

From *"Dictionary of Bird Totems"* in *Animal Speak* BY TED ANDREWS

. . . .

November, 1993

Penetanguishene "Naval and Military Establishments" [in central Ontario]: just arrived at this historical site, to do a week of performances based on *Eleanora's Diary*, tired, anxious.... The most significant part of getting here was a heron, literally standing beside the road just a few yards from the car as we drove down a small side road. It was a total surprise, so late in the season, on such a frosty morning! By rights, we should not even have been there because we had made a wrong turning. But there we were and there she was! She didn't move as we passed, just fixed her eye, yellow and beady, on us. I felt deeply startled.

Stop! Be still and silent!
See the great blue heron there?
Standing like a sentinel among the willow roots
(Roots arranged in order, a long-abandoned border)
— will he stay and keep on watching, beady-eyed?
He spots me with his yellow eye....

Excerpt from my poem *Over the Fence*

We only glimpsed that roadside heron for a minute, and yet our encounter seemed enormous. Her staring eye seemed to convey a flash of inquisition, boring into me. I felt more confronted than contemplative, as if the heron's sharp yellow glance encompassed all my foibles and failings, regrets, anxieties and personal wrong turnings! Powerful responses welled up in me, and then she was behind us.

When I told my friend Sandy about this incident, she said the heron was probably a messenger, but I sensed no particular message, aside from feeling alarmed by a heron that was simply standing sentinel, aside from remembering my discomfort as I met that heron's beady stare. Yet I recall that Euripides said "Birds are messengers of the Gods," and I keep searching for meaning.

Perhaps that startling, all-seeing heron on the roadside reflected my ongoing uneasiness about myself and my life with David. It could even be that the intensity I experienced in passing the heron was a push to let myself be more open and receptive to my inner self. Taking the time to be as still as the sharp-eyed heron may mean focusing more deeply than I usually do.

Oh Great Spirit, help me to stare into the depths of being without flinching.

. . . .

(likely winter 1993-94)

... Talked to Sandy in Toronto, who says she can see that we have no "slack" for each other just now, and that David is wound tighter than tight. I put it to him later as "We aren't giving each other any grace." (Oh help me be gracious!)

Sunday, 23rd January 1994, bedtime (sleepy)

Just a minute to <u>nota bene</u> a wonderful happening today with David. At the table he gave me a kiss and hug with a glimmer of our former enthusiasm — a real longing for each other (only a glimmer, yet it was so <u>much</u> to me). The feeling of truly loving David that I had forgotten! Just a glimpse, but so hopeful-making.

31st May 1994

... Consumed with angst about my upcoming 49th birthday, I set up a counselling session. Then I raced out for a run with Jessie before going. What did I see but one heron flying far off over Mud Lake and then a pair of them, near the straight path between the river and the road! Seeing the <u>three</u> of them, I felt I could carry on, glad of their benison.

6th June 1994

... David came home three days ago and confided that he had cried for almost the whole hour at his counsellor's. An Englishman in tears — how rare! Since then we have just had a remarkable ease between us, and I have felt immersed in the flow of life, with a sense of everlasting spirit housed in these beautiful but transitory human bodies. Heaven only knows whether it's his movement or mine....

23rd June 1994

Two herons met out over the blue ground of the river. For a moment they flew together, wings parallel, doing a slow bird dance around one another. Then their flight paths widened, and they set off in different directions, while I stood weeping with a sense of timeless joy.

Grey herons rising
          wings spread wide, like our spirits,
               Greeting, saluting.

The primeval rhythms of the seashore. Rollers on the beach, wind in the pines, the slow flapping herons across sand dunes.

Gift from the Sea BY ANNE MORROW LINDBERGH

How challenging to let our long term relationships evolve, especially marriages! Seeing the herons around our home in Britannia — signals to remember the Great Spirit — inspired me. Watching two herons circle each other along the river or lake repeatedly helped me take the long view. These graceful creatures communing together modelled for me what David and I could be with one another.

Ours was a slow, often frustrating evolution, as these journal dates spiralled through several years reflect. Yet the herons continued to chronicle moments of profound spiritual connection for me. They offered a timeless, mystical counterpoint to our attempt to balance our relationship.

I think of the herons' parallel dances as visual translations of Rilke's observation, which I have treasured for years: "Love consists in this, that two solitudes border and protect and salute one another."

· ·

July 1994

... Traveled home through New England easily, after a spirit-deepening Quaker week. It's the third such "Gathering" my daughter, son and I have attended together.

I felt very spiritually refreshed and saw at least five herons en route! One was high above us; later another flew directly over the car, its S-shaped neck and pointed beak so close I was astounded. That big heron flew in the same direction as we were driving for a few timeless seconds, as if protecting or guiding us. My heart sang with gratitude beneath that wide, pulsing wingspan, that Largeness.

Herons do seem to be my sacred bird — they surely ARE a way in which I find myself attuned to life's Mystery! Or is it that they find me? No matter, I am happy to coexist with their mystery.

Mystery is the depth of the sacred.

Coming Home to Myself by MARION WOODMAN

· ·

August 1994

Evening in Quebec, on the way back from Nova Scotia, we stopped at a lovely old auberge right on the St. Lawrence, near Riviere du Loup.... Late sunlight streamed through the big windows beside us, and no sooner had we sat down to supper than my driving companion saw a heron outside the window. I turned to look, and saw another! They stayed still-standing, then tall-stalking along the shore for some time, while we ate. The tide was coming in, and I guess the first one must have taken off without my noticing his departure. Near the end of our meal, the remaining huge heron rose on his wings to fly towards us as we watched from the sunset-filled dining room. He settled briefly on the beach just outside our window, and then flew off — as if he had come to say goodbye.

After supper, walking westward up the beach in that heron's wake, I soon spotted him way up ahead on a rock. We ambled on to where he was hunched in a very grandfather-of-all-herons position, shared a few minutes of silence with him, and then returned to the car. As we drove by the same spot again, he was flying along towards us into the dusk. A little further on I saw two more herons close together on another big rock, dimly silhouetted against the darkening sky.

I'd call it a six heron evening, but it had more continuity than that, felt like a bird benison, an unplanned-for-enrichment to my travels. I realized herons have marked each of my transitions home this summer! This is the third set of herons glimpsed on a return journey, and each has been a remarkable gift, grounding me with a sense of Spirit.

> *... The 'spiritual' is not something other-worldly but a deepening appreciation*
> *of the sacredness, the miraculousness of the present moment.*
>
> *A Faith To Call Our Own* BY ALEX WILDWOOD

It seems a simple truth that holidays can give us a miraculous change of focus. However, coming home after these times of renewal, I struggle to resume daily routines while staying in tune to Spirit. How tricky to shift my mental and emotional gears; how many loose ends! The gift of seeing herons as I travel home eases the process. Herons live on the edges of the land and water worlds, and feed both above and below water, so perhaps they can truly be called birds of transition. I have also read that in Celtic mythology birds were honoured as travellers between the living world and the world of the dead.

Oh Great Mystery,

each time I travel homeward,

preparing to re-engage with my daily life,

help me to move as gracefully as

these goliath birds of your creation.

May I remember to be still in spirit

and make my transitions as the herons seem to,

with patience, deliberation and elegance.

. . . .

August 1994

… While I was away at [Quaker] Yearly Meeting in Nova Scotia, I signed up for a group discussion about prayer. Eight of us, of whom several were very dear Friends and wise older women, gathered for a close and precious time.

The leader opened our session by saying he didn't know what the boundaries of prayer were, and to my dismay quiet tears overwhelmed me. I still felt fragile when it was my turn to share my thoughts. Nonetheless I chose to be open and to tell them about "my" herons. I spoke specifically about one summer day on the bike path, when I had seen herons in an abundance that electrified me, and I said, "Whatever it means, I pray with herons."

. . . .

Sometimes,

when it is all, finally,

too much,

I climb into my car,

roll the windows up,

and somewhere between

backing out the driveway

and rounding the first corner,

I let out a yell

that would topple Manhattan.

How do you pray?

Untitled poem BY MARGARET L. MITCHELL in *Ms.* magazine, December 1987

W hat I have been learning over these heron years is that part of being truly human is to pray, even though I don't think I fully understand what prayer is. In that Quaker group in 1994, I said I couldn't comprehend it fully, but knew in some strong inner way that I pray in the presence of herons, or through them. I remember the sense that this sharing was seminal, was a turning point in my life.

In another Quaker group the leader referred to prayer as "absolute attention." That description of prayer makes profound sense to me. When I am giving thanks or seeking help for myself or others, the more I am totally absorbed in that process, the more connected to the Divine Spirit I feel. When I experience herons — for reasons beyond my understanding — I am attentive in the deepest ways I know.

... And herefore it is written, that short prayer pierceth heaven....
Surely because it is prayed with full spirit, in the height and in the deepness,
in the length and in the breadth of his spirit that prayeth it....
Prayer in itself properly is not else, but a devout intent
direct unto God for getting of good and removing of evil....
And if we will intentively pray for getting of good, let us cry,
either with word or with thought or with desire,
not else nor no more words, but this word, "God."

The Cloud of Unknowing BY UNKNOWN 15th CENTURY AUTHOR

· ·

15th September 1994

Last night, the fourth evening since David's return from a week on retreat by himself, we had a satisfying walk and talk on the beach. We were blessed by a heron flying across our view to poise in the bay. Its slow black silhouette shimmered against the pastel water and orange sunset sky.

That heron wading among the evening ducks seemed like an ally, a spiritual presence, and I tried to listen inwardly as we walked. I exploded at David briefly, but we did reach some practical agreements about our life together now, as we struggle to reshape it after so many years. I think we both agree to stay together till our son is launched, for one BIG thing....

20th September 1994

I woke up feeling pretty delicious! There's a lot to report on in the last five very intense days.... I had a counselling session during which I took off my wedding ring, resolved to put it back on only when it symbolizes a *new* relationship with David, not old patterns.... I think I am defining my boundaries ... plus, *two* great blue herons flew over me on Saturday! Quonking and surging, their message seemed to be "Courage!"

1st October 1994

I'm getting used to saying, "I pray with herons," and "I hang out with herons" — now also "I cry with herons!" Today I just stood on my lookout point and watched the same big fellow I had seen fly across the lake earlier, and felt thankful he was there ... and wept.

At first I thought about what I have come to hold as the symbolism of herons — whether flying purposefully, or standing still, or moving and feeding. Then I was crying, remembering the deep truth I had found in a recent counselling session: MY LIFE IS THIS HARD/WAS THIS HARD. After about five minutes of big tears, my sense of those words seemed to evolve to: THIS IS AS HARD AS IT WILL GET/CAN BE.

I understood that working on my relationship to David feels harder than anything I have ever experienced, but I have become very clear about my own needs and value. So it's not going to get any harder. I am engaged with the struggle, and it's challenging, yet good to make this raw recognition.

· ·

Hokusai says look carefully
He says pay attention, notice
He says keep looking, stay curious
He says there is no end to seeing.
He says look forward to getting old

He says keep changing, you just keep getting more who you really are
He says get stuck, accept it, repeat yourself
As long as it's interesting
He says keep doing what you love.
He says keep praying....

Excerpt from *Hokusai Says* by ROGER KEYES

· ·

8th January 1995

FEAR NOT, FOR I AM WITH YOU — LO, I AM WITH YOU ALWAYS, EVEN UNTO THE ENDS OF THE EARTH. These words have been very satisfyingly with me since I woke. The sky outside my window is a deep, deep turquoise colour, sliced by the beautiful vertical lines of more than ten big icicles, gleaming in the cold street light.... I have been afraid to look forward, to trust in the mystery we label "God," or to accept myself as a reflection of Goddess, with Divine gifts to share.

· ·

What do I mean by prayer? I mean the practice of relatedness.
On one side, prayer is our capacity to enter into that vast community
of life in which self and other, human and non-human, visible and
invisible, are intricately intertwined. While my senses discriminate
and my mind dissects, my prayer acknowledges and recreates the unity
of life... knowing the transcendent center that connects us all.

To Know As We Are Known: Education As A Spiritual Journey
BY PARKER PALMER

Those years in the early 90s were such an emotional time, when my spiritual life was also deepening. I had my heron experiences, for sure, and felt intensely touched and uplifted by them. And, I had embarked on *The Artist's Way* course in May of 1994, savouring its many self-reflective exercises.

In January 1995 I had my turquoise dawn message of "Fear not!", which stirred me so. That spring I had a special opportunity to survey my spiritual history. I was asked to represent Quakers in a TV documentary series about different faith communities. I had

never taken the time to think about the evolution and chronology of my spiritual life. The interview experience with Ann, a lay nun, was a kind of soul history. I spent hours talking to her about my spiritual beginnings and growth, coming to see there was an important way in which herons were woven into my whole story.

Our final interview actually took place along a placid margin of Britannia Bay. One misty June morning I biked to the area we had chosen, watched a heron fishing in a shallow pool busy with other waterfowl, and waited for the TV crew. I said what I call my prayers in quiet communion with the heron (these are a set of written-out affirmations, reminders, and bits of gleaned wisdom I try to recite by heart). When the heron flapped slowly off upriver, and no TV van had driven up, I biked home to reconfirm our meeting place. They finally arrived, and the heron did return, but — ironically — they never managed to photograph him! In the end the documentary used some still photos spliced in between shots of me seated beside a long sandy spit, explaining my journey with the herons.

... Because I am never out of the lap of the Buddha,

never out of the hands of the Teacher,

never apart from Divine Oneness

except as I forget and can repeatedly remember,

I can leap, and the Net will appear;

I can rest on the divine waters or soar with the sacred winds of change,

trusting I am always undergirded and supported. ...

From one of my prayers based on ideas in *The Artist's Way*

After life in Ottawa settled into familiarity and my second book for young people was published, I was unclear about what next career steps to take. I experimented with several writing projects, always aware that my family needed more income. Not only was I unsure of my work, but my marriage seemed to be mired in frustration and misunderstanding, There were shifts happening on many levels, and yet I felt stuck in several ways.

Paradoxically there were also times of heron attunement and other moments of deep knowing, of sensing spiritual truths. Ten years later, I told a Unitarian Universalist colleague how contributing to that 1995 documentary was a milestone. Telling Ann and the TV camera about "my" herons showed me I had reached a point where I could speak openly and relaxedly about them. From then on I simply referred to herons, seen or unseen, as spiritual companions. I often say they serve as flags for, or windows into, moments of intense meaning for me.

Spirit of the Wind

Original words and melody BY STAR WILLIAMS. Heron verse BY CBP.

Spi-rit of the wind, car - ry me! Spi-rit of the wind, car - ry me home.

Spi-rit of the wind, car - ry me home,____ to my- self.____

Spi-rit of the he- ron, hold me past all bear- ing; Spi-rit of wide wings, help__ my soul to sing.

____ Spi-rit of the wind, car - ry me! Spi-rit of the wind, car - ry me home.

Spi-rit of the wind, car - ry me home,____ to my- self._____

. . . .

Sunday, 30th October 1994

A beautiful balmy day — such a gift this late in the year! … I've felt quite spiritually in tune all day, as if any moment a heron might fly over (and they often do!). David and I spent time in the garden together; it's good for him to just be physical outdoors after all his work stresses, good for us both!

Monday night, 8th November 1994

I came back yesterday from a wonderful trip to Toronto. Talking to Sandy there again, she gave a very useful name to my frustration about money, love and work. "So," she said, "You're in the 'I don't know' place." Somehow naming it is more honourable, makes the fact of my lack of clarity, of my anger about "WHY doesn't Way open?" less frustrating. I'm simply there, in the "I don't know place."…

I had a nice surprise of a bigger fall royalty cheque for *Let's Celebrate!* than last year, plus I am carving out a little niche for myself at the *Ottawa Citizen*, writing their Kids' Page once a month — for a fee!

16th November 1994

On a cold, raw morning, I assumed the herons had quite sensibly decided to go south, but no — I saw two: one standing mid-lake, and one near the road. Both were hunched into themselves, feathers fluffed out as insulation from the chilly damp. Both of them flew up and away when I got too close, yet they were motionless long enough for me to stand and "be" with them. That yielded an awareness of being still and knowing God, whatever is going on.

When I am upset or panicky, this knowing is a kind of bottom line that I long for. Although I don't usually think of the Divine as something solid, in this mental place, I need Spirit to be dense; I need a solid, rock-bottom resting place in Spirit, unchanging, more deeply rooted than my favourite great oak trees, calmer than the quietest water. Maybe this is the "firm foundation" in the old hymns.

. . . .

From as early as I can remember, praying was something quite different
from praying in church. It was always being alone in nature — under a tree,
in a tree, under a bush, digging a hole, walking with my dogs,
watching birds, listening to the river.

MEINRAD CRAIGHEAD quoted in *The Feminine Face of God*

Spirit can be a firm foundation, can be that strong, yes — but the images of rock or wall no longer quite fit. My mind scans memories of leaning on my beloved grandfather tree, or memories of serenity when I stand beside a reflecting bay of a lake or river. What comes next to mind are the strong, encircling arms of people who love me, or the balanced embrace of a good dance partner. Sometimes I dance with a person who just emanates a solid, grounded quality, or I share long hugs with dear ones, and I so enjoy receiving them. I realize that what some refer to as "the Everlasting Arms" are more strongly loving than even these human experiences.

A huge feathered bird, rising from a murky swamp, doesn't seem to be the same as a caring pair of arms. Yet when I see the motionless profile of a patient heron, my thoughts move on from the knowledge that the Sacred is somehow my still point, spiral on through a consciousness of Spirit as bedrock, to an awareness of being held while growing, being safe while taking risks. Above all, I rejoice in a sense of being encouraged and cherished by the Divine arms — or Divine wings!

Some years after writing the journal entries and the previous reflection, I watched a video interview with an Orthodox rabbi who declared, "Often the holiest place to be *is* the place of being stuck and not knowing what to do." I was so stunned by his words that I had to run the sequence over and over again, to get my Quaker/Protestant head and heart to understand Rabbi Steven Greenberg fully. He went on to explain that, "Unlike other religions where beatitude and calm and certain faith are the core of the religious experience, [in Judaism] debate and uncertainty and challenge" are central. He even said that for Jews "God revels in our struggle to make sense of our world and ourselves...."

What a radical attitude! To me, my "I don't know place" has been a very uncomfortable if not hellish place, a state of mind to get out of as soon as I can. But what if it is holy? What if this Quaker process of "waiting patiently for Way to open" is not simply to be endured, but welcomed? What a phenomenal, completely different point of view for me! As a woman in midlife who almost relentlessly seeks stillness and a sense of Divine purpose, can I shift my perspective to welcome my inner struggles? At the very least, can I stop feeling that my inward uncertainty is somehow bad? O Great Mystery, help me not only to "wait patiently ..." but to enjoy — even revel! — in my human condition, to know I am engaged with the holy.

There is no word in English for not being certain.
We have only the negative "uncertainty." Apparently the
condition of uncertainty is not sufficiently pervasive in our
thinking to require a name. We have "misery" for unhappiness,
"mess" for untidiness ... [but nothing that] conveys the simple
opposite of certainty, a condition marked not by puzzlement,
anxiety or frustration, but by confidence — even excitement —
at the fact that we really don't know.

The Fatal Flaw BY DUNCAN HOWLETT

Before and After

As this Spiral unwinds, I curl back through journal entries from the summers of 1993 and '94, noting my inner learnings and growth. Life seemed such a see-saw! Days both calm and crazy spiralled on into 1995. By June I was again at work on trust — a lifelong project — and then my journal halted abruptly, to resume later with a number of sleepless middle-of-the-night entries.

My hope is that by telling my story, you will find the courage to trust your own voice — to listen to what your soul is trying to tell you. If you are willing to trust, to have faith in the unfolding, we can go on this journey together. Together we can stretch — and dare to be as big as we really are.

Stretching Lessons: The Daring That Starts from Within BY SUE BENDER

. . . .

August 1993

Hot summer evening: my canoeing buddy came over to go paddling round Mud Lake … a peaceful sunset trip, the water fairly still except for the ripples we made, and we collected a whole clutch of wonderful feathers. I think they are all from herons: big and stiff or fluffy and smaller, variegated or blue-grey — lots! We also were absorbed in watching herons and spoke softly, pointing out each new sighting, steering around stumps and snags, aiming towards the various trees we could see the herons chose to roost in. The whole trip seemed special, whether we were gazing across the lake, dipping our paddles into its glassy surface, or gathering up yet another feather in the beautiful rosy light. We may only have spent an hour, but it seemed like a blissful eternity.

The heron used the feathers on the tips of his wings — his hand section — somewhat like propellers. As he flapped along, his wing tips went forward and down, up and back, in countless figure eights.

A Solitary Blue BY CYNTHIA VOIGT

After that reverent evening, I put all the feathers in a shiny brass cup, like a bouquet of grey-blue-white-black textures, to help me remember that sacred-seeming time, help me recall herons even when it's no longer heron season, or not a heron day. Some while later I took a few feathers out of the bunch I had gathered, to spread their heron presence around. A little cluster of soft breast plumage is a part of my earring collection now, and one big quill is in my daily journal pages folder, a constant invocation. I tucked one of the smaller feathers, dramatically half black, half white, into my wallet. It served as a delicate sign of the big birds that remind me of the Divine. Eventually I found a special use for this particular feather.

Perhaps a year after my feather-gathering canoe trip, I was traveling further afield. My son, who shares my pleasure in writing poetry, stopped with me to visit the grave of Emily Dickinson, the reclusive poet, in Amherst, Massachusetts. The old burial ground there is a place of pilgrimage, and her gravestone is often decked with small symbols of homage — pebbles and flowers, shells, even poems. When I told my son he might like to leave his own gift, he got out a precious black crow feather given by a friend, and stuck its stiff shaft in the edge of soil and grass at the bottom of Emily's white marble headstone.

As he did so, I remembered the heron feather in my wallet and planted it beside my son's crow token. We stood there together in the quiet burial ground in silence for a few minutes. The image of Dickinson's narrow white stone, with several other little offerings perched on the top and our two gestures at its green foot, became increasingly potent. I was aware of the whole area coming to be a holy space, almost a church without walls. A palpable sense of worship and blessing hovered around us, as if honouring Emily thus connected us to a whole host of others who loved her work, as if those two small feathers had evoked the very wings of Spirit.

– Salute to poetry –
Myself, my son – both poets, too –
Reached through that silent fence
To place a precious feather: each
A symbol of our need
To hear (or be) with – herons – crows
– and Emily – winged eternity.

Excerpt from my poem *Grave Gifts — in Homage to Emily Dickinson*

. . . .

Summer 1993 or 1994

On the high rocks overlooking the south end of Mud Lake: Oh growl! The heron I was watching while I wrote in my journal here flew off without my noticing. I am cross both because I didn't sense his leaving and also because I didn't get to see his reflection — in the mirror-lake of today — as he went. Still, he appeared after I had searched the waterscape before me in vain, so I wish I could just accept that now he's also gone, equally without warning.

The heron's appearance and disappearance reminds me of Spirit, of how sometimes I am surprised by a consciousness of Spirit that just descends upon me, unannounced. I remember, too, hearing reference to Carl Jung's grave. Apparently he specified that his headstone would read, "Summoned or not, Spirit is present." Similarly, so it is with herons…. There! I glimpsed the heron rise and flap off to a new watching post in the swamp buttonwood. I can't see him just at this minute, but I know he is there, and will show himself again. How often I re-experience this lesson.

I became aware that I could be healed and could bring about healing in myself and others … by being there, by willing my energies in that direction, by being open, by letting life flow and occasionally surge through me, unlocked and free.

Telling Our Stories BY ALISON LEONARD

One fall day in the early 90s, I was surprised by the sudden fluttering appearance of a chickadee, right in front of my face, when I was actually looking for herons. I had been jogging round Mud Lake, and although it was getting late in the autumn, I was still heron-checking the swamp area. To my delight, a tiny chickadee flew up and then hovered between my outstretched hands. Intuitively, I understood that his tribe, the cheery chickadees, would be staying in frozen Ontario right through the winter, and that even though the herons would fly south, these little foragers would keep me company, would stand in for the great herons until their return, usually in early April.

After that intriguing encounter, there were several times when chickadees surrounded me in the bush, or flew down to investigate the seeds held out in my hand. They were a friendly bird benediction, little grace notes in the winter cold.

Then there came a day when I truly summoned the chickadees. I had been walking with my dear friend Chris and our dogs through the snowy woods and out across the ice, and she was deeply upset about a disagreement she had had with some colleagues. I couldn't seem to ease her mind, no matter what I said, and finally I leaned against a great oak tree and breathed out a fervent prayer to Spirit and to the chickadees to come to our aid. Mysteriously, several zoomed down, pecking at crumbs in Chris's hands, clinging to her fingers with their tiny claws: small black-capped distractions.

A miraculous few minutes passed, and then the buoyant chickadees flew on. My friend was profoundly comforted by their contact. They would not alight on my hands that time, only hers, and the next day when I tried to call them just out of curiosity, they flew near but never deigned to touch me. There's no way to explain such a descent of birds — and Holy Mystery — as Chris and I experienced. Still, those chickadees did seem to be feathered agents of the Spirit, ready to be summoned, as Jung famously observed.

Into the blur of tears
flit
flick
flit
sibilant flutter
of small grey wings
chip
chip chip
chickadee-dee-dee-dee-dee
beyond the tiny clasp
their presence seems weightless
on my fingers
yet what prodigious weights they lift
from the heart ...

Excerpt from *Chickadee Epiphany* by CHRISTINA MACEWAN

*In essence, prayer is communion with mystery.... The more we
come alive and awake, the more everything we do becomes prayer.*

Gratefullness, the Heart of Prayer by BROTHER DAVID STEINDL-RAST

. . . .

August 1994 at NeeKauNis (a Quaker camp in central Ontario)
... Watching some little children play quietly nearby, I thought about the way the camp
community nurtures them all, how we all share the parenting. Next, I pondered the
question of whether my husband and I had ever fully allowed, let alone truly encouraged,
each other to stretch ourselves to be our most whole selves. I thought we seemed to have
succeeded with our son and daughter, but hardly ever as partners.... Then I felt a prayer
rise in me, that we adults may help each other, and each young one especially, stretch
his or her wings fully, that we not inhibit, but enhance one another. I felt this longing
very deeply, and wide-winged heron images flooded my mind, almost as if they were
surrounding me in Spirit, vividly present although not physically visible.

. . . .

*Love really has just that one absolute, implacable demand,
... to desire the achievement of wholeness by the beloved.*

Marriage and Other Acts of Charity by KATE BRAESTRUP

At Camp NeeKauNis, where my children and I love to spend a summer week or
two, we sit in Meeting for Worship on the hill high above the broad lake every
morning. That quiet half hour which I journaled about, when I was overwhelmed with
a powerful sense of herons, has stayed with me especially. Back at home, I went dog
walking (and of course talking) with my friend Chris-of-the-chickadee descent. When I
mentioned this intense experience I had had at camp, feeling so many invisible herons
around me, thinking about spreading my own "heron wings," she looked startled, and
asked me more specifically when that had happened. It turned out she herself had had a
strong consciousness of me, at that very hour, and had been astounded to then see not
one but five real herons — and had written a poem about them!

CAROLINE'S HERON [excerpt]

I have come again to the healing place
Where the river rounds over the stones
and wraps around the willow roots....
A heron appears, flying high.
Caroline has sent me
Her heron.
Since she cannot be here.
But of course, she is here;
There's the heron.
What?
Four more?
No

Can't be
But yes! Five great blue herons
flying... high.
Conversing across the sky.
One detaches itself, overflies.
Bird book silhouette
Descends.
The early sunlight
Glints on the pale silvery neck
As it arches to one side... to the other.
One short hoarse croak and it rises again
Its huge wings primordial in their ponderous grace.
There are gods: many and one; healing laps
in their wings.
And power.
Gifts of love.

BY CHRISTINA MACEWAN

What powerful gifts my time of worship filled with herons, and then Chris's poem, were to me, although I know this synchronicity is inexplicable. I can only be amazed myself, giving thanks for our friendship and for the many ways this dear woman has nurtured me, sharing healing times, words — and herons.

When we answer that call [to our deepest selves] ... we set in motion the principle that C. G. Jung dubbed synchronicity, loosely defined as a fortuitous intermeshing of events.

The Artist's Way BY JULIA CAMERON

. . . .

Late August 1994

Today David and I went to and from Grosse Isle, now so inactive a site, yet so heavy with history. We travelled along the St. Lawrence River to the little immigration island in a bumpy water taxi, its noisy engine and high wake disturbing numerous birds. And there were herons, too, standing in the sleepy coves and marshes of the island, oblivious of our human coming and going. The herons must have been similarly unconcerned with all the 19th Century emigrants who once alighted on this island's rocky shores. Many of those settlers died of exhaustion or cholera, and their bodies sleep there rather than on the mainland they sought. Their ghosts felt almost palpable to me as we wandered along dusty paths, through the old hostels and past sun-baked sheds.

The herons were a bonus today, and I was very pleased to see so many, although overall I did not have such strongly spirit-stirring experiences of them as heretofore — perhaps because I was out in the world with David and the other visitors, rather than alone.

However, this morning before beginning what became my adventure with David, standing by myself with my hands prayerfully open to the energy of the day, to Spirit, an initial heron did appear as if on cue. I was on the edge of a wind-rippled marsh, by a big old Catholic church in the village where we stayed, gazing out from a little octagonal gazebo with a cross on top, when that first heron flapped slowly across the green reeds. And then there were simply more and more herons all day, a winged emphasis to all the richness of the trip.

... He watched the graceful, powerful poetry of measured wingbeats until the heron was out of sight.

Great Blue, the Odyssey of a Great Blue Heron BY MARNIE REED CROWELL

How is it that the stresses and strains of marriage, which after a number of years can seem like dry cracks in parched earth, sometimes split further, into yawning chasms? In 1994, when David and I were labouring to bridge some bewildering gaps in our relationship of over twenty-six years, we shared a wonderful, yet difficult summer outing. We met in Quebec, after some individual holiday times, and went to see the national historic site at Grosse Isle on the St. Lawrence. I think we both feared that it might be the day we decided to separate, but that fate was never voiced.

Later we had an extremely elegant five course dinner together to celebrate a big royalty cheque for my book, *Eleanora's Diary*. As we dined we tried to recall all the other special occasions when we had feasted like that, and with whom, or where and why. We laughed and felt briefly in tune. In my journal, I wrote of being glad to remember the abundance of the past, even as we strained to see our life together in the present as not arid, struggled not to desert each other in our hearts.

I also wrote about my own epiphany of seeing eight or nine herons that day — the most I had ever seen over one day at that time. David and I had much common interest in Grosse Isle Park itself, and it was good to share our exploration of its paths and buildings, forgotten graves and abandoned objects. Thinking back over the day, I don't remember how much of my spiritual pleasure in spotting the herons I was also able to share with him; my moments of heron communion have usually been quite private.

Nonetheless I do recall that ten months later we watched a heron together in a mood of unspoken worship. We took a ferry across Lake Champlain that June day and leaned on the railing side by side, silently tracking another huge bird. It flew across our bow once, and back past us again, then continued steadily off over the smoky blue waters until it was a tiny flapping speck, and finally gone.

That great blue heron with its far-reaching wingspan did not actually disappear into the blue, though that was our impression. Like so many things to do with perspective, when we could no longer see the heron, it was becoming visible to new watchers, to those standing at different vantage points around the lake. I rejoiced to share that wordless heron meditation with my husband.

. . . .

8th January 1995

... I have been afraid rather more than usually, in the face of all I have to do in terms of work and travel over the next four or five months.... But this morning I feel clear that I am called to continue to listen to my body and not try to do everything; to rest more ... and to "fear not, and know that I am God." ... Part of the lesson just may be that I myself am part of the great unknown we label "God," a reflection of God, with Divine gifts to share.

> *There is a mystery that animates every living thing,*
> *a mystery that sustains what we call life....*
>
> *Some call this mystery, the source of life, the Ground of Being,*
> *the creative force, the spirit of life or God.*
>
> *Some do not know what to call this mystery*
> *and leave it nameless....*

Excerpt from the meditation *"The Flame and the Mystery"* BY EDWARD SEARL
in *Fulfilling a Dream / Vers un rêve à bâtir*

The winter-spring of 1995 was an intense period for our family, beginning with a car accident which unnerved us all despite no one being hurt, but proved fortuitous in terms of insurance. I was preoccupied with some new school projects plus concerts, meetings and travel to Pennsylvania. My book was doing well, though presentations about it meant I had too full a schedule for much reflection. On David's part, there were ugly budget cuts and administrative changes going on at the museum, which he only spoke of tersely, and he had conferences to travel to, while often feeling inexplicably unwell. At Easter time we planned to attend our niece's wedding in England. David and I continued to wrestle with questions of how to communicate honestly or to share our domestic and parenting routines effectively. Money was still an issue, yet I could only erratically address possible writing projects. In late March I experimented with a personal narrative in the present-tense that I thought I might submit as a radio essay.

Between the growth and the gravel,
I shall do something
to make the world more beautiful.

From the poem for Miss Rumphius in *Out of the Skin, Into the Soul: The Art of Aging* by DOROTHY ALBRACHT DOHERTY AND MARY COLGAN McNAMARA

One winter-ending-soon day I go jogging in a gingerly fashion across the dead grass and brown mud that will become the summer lawn of the filtration plant. I note there are only a few patches of snow left, around the edges of the open area. My feet slip a bit on the mud that has thawed in the sunlight, and then — WHOOPS! I trip on the edge of the curb and sprawl into the small supply road.

Luckily, there's no traffic. Somehow I decide to just lie there and be aware of having fallen down, to cry out "Ow, it hurts!" for my grazed palm, banged elbow, perhaps skinned knee — and inner confusion. I don't get up, simply feel those hurts. I can see that the heel of my right hand is bleeding a little, and I brush the gravel off, then just bawl, bawl for my knee that smarts inside my corduroys, bawl for how I often seem to hurt myself when my spirit feels off balance, when some part of my life is askew.

Tears continue to spill into my scarf as I push my body up from the almost warm black pavement; when I wipe my eyes, I catch a glimpse of an approaching van, so I limp onwards. The driver calls out, "Are you all right?" and I nod, heading farther across the dun-coloured grass. Yes, I am okay to keep moving, my scrapes don't feel too serious, but my fall tells me I am body and heartsore; I won't run more today. However, I still want to go check out the river channel, the place where it runs deep and fast between the shore and a long island ridge below the rapids. I want to see how much ice is left there, and if there are any winter ducks about.

To get there, I have to negotiate an icy path, and I move very carefully, though my sight is blurred with the tears that won't stop flowing. I pick my way between bare bushes towards the rushing water; here and there my feet break through the rotten ice which coats the pathway. Sometimes I choose to traverse a few low corn-coarse snow piles instead. Other times a wet, shiny bit of rock shelf presents itself for more stable footing. Pretty sure I am alone, I still feel like howling, and shout, "Ow! OW! OOOWW!" as I rub my knee and elbow.

I cross a few more stoney yards of snow and ice to find myself swearing out loud at the river. "Damn! Why do I have to hurt this much? Why is there all this pain? OWWW!" Suddenly I realize my curses are being absorbed by more than the dark flowing water: two surprised-looking Canada geese are paddling hard in my direction, trying to get free enough of the current to come close and see if I have brought them any food. My stormy protests momentarily change to laughter — no herons in this early springtime, but some other familiar big birds have appeared to keep me company. Well, I don't have any seed, and I hurt! So I keep shouting, keep giving voice to my frustration, but the geese don't seem to mind, just keep working their webbed feet hard to stay near.

"What do you know, geese?" I sneer. "You don't have to fix a marriage and figure out how to earn a better living, you don't have to keep asking yourself and the Great Spirit what's the best next move, while working so much there's no time to listen! I cannot see what to do differently or better! I feel stuck — so much so I nearly got stuck in that mud — and then I fell face down, right into my sense of misery! You silly geese may be smarter than I think: you at least know when it's time to go south, and when to return."

I don't know what to do, except to say that I'm out of kilter, conscious that I'm hurting; don't know if I'll ever get finished with this despair, or vanquish my howls for all time. But I know by my watch that now it's time to turn away homewards; I know by the stronger sunlight that the season is turning. The geese keep paddling hopefully, and I stop my tirade, muster a wry smile. The herons will return soon, and so will my sense of faith and well-being. I do know these homely realities to be true: after the winter comes the spring, and joy and light break through after our dark inner storms.

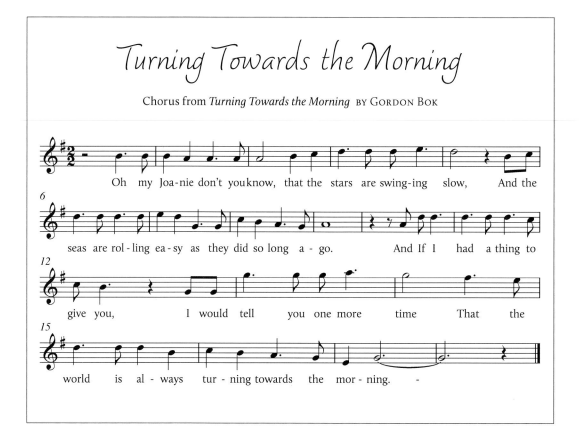

Turning Towards the Morning

Chorus from *Turning Towards the Morning* BY GORDON BOK

Oh my Joa-nie don't you know, that the stars are swing-ing slow, And the seas are rol-ling ea-sy as they did so long a-go. And If I had a thing to give you, I would tell you one more time That the world is al-ways tur-ning towards the mor-ning. -

· ·

April 1995

[all of us in Britain on vacation with David's sister's family]

... As we were driving back to Hertfordshire from the Black Mountains in Wales, I saw a European grey heron in the evening light, flying in the opposite direction to the car — an unanticipated enrichment!

Like the heron, now I also fly — home to Canada today. David and the children returned a few days ago, leaving me free to explore Worcestershire and do some networking. Yesterday another heron went winging by at sunset, just above the road! In addition, when I was walking down a quiet lane, I saw a plastic heron standing in a garden pool. It was lifelike enough to fool me briefly — then the wind made it vibrate unrealistically. For an instant it was like that moment when you think you've caught sight of some very dear person in a crowd, and your heart skips, but then they're gone, you realize it's someone else.... How wonderful to have seen the two real herons — and even the silly fake one — here, giving me a glimpse that all is well and Spirit is with me in England, in Canada, wherever I may be.

I feel renewed by all the nature experiences we have had on this holiday. How I have revelled in the sun and air and green countryside!

....

May 1995

[back in Ottawa] ...Today after struggling at my desk with money business that makes me feel so confused, I gave myself a sunny afternoon treat and went running. And what should I see but a heron, standing quite near me for a long time! Finally he flew off, quonking, and when I went to the lookout point and saw him standing again, a second one flew by with its distinctive wing movements, ponderous yet beautiful!

I cried as I watched them — tears for my need to trust that especially when I feel overwhelmed and unable to cope, I am in the hand of God, in the lap of the Buddha. I want to know this reality fully, from my toes to my finger (wing?) tips, and it's hard to hold onto. Just when I most need to remember the Divine, that I am always partnered, I often fret or fume about no time or money, about all there is to do. I start to pick at myself for all sorts of self-judged inadequacies, and that's a cycle I have trouble breaking, though the herons help.

....

Learning to trust the unfolding of one's own life is awkward,
painful work that often leaves one feeling exposed and vulnerable.

The Feminine Face of God by SHERRY RUTH ANDERSON AND PATRICIA HOPKINS

. . . .

4th June 1995

Almost my 50th birthday.... Sitting in an outdoor worship circle, speaking into the green leafy quiet, I articulate that this is the period of my life when I am learning about trust, about all the help that is out there, both Divine and human. Paradoxically, after a half century of striving to be "a big girl," I am learning about interdependence, even as I live in a culture that teaches us the false virtue of independence. We are told to be strong, made to think "I should do it all" when the deepest spiritual reality is more that we are all held in an unmeasurable Divine net, and we get to work on our own unique pieces of that huge whole, alongside countless others, seen and unseen. My place seems to be standing with herons!

. . . .

I have had to rebuild a concept of trust that...emerges in the middle of my dialogue with life, in the middle of my doubts, fears, questions, and offers me another chance to choose to have faith in the hubbub, not to deaden my sense of reality. Trust is the decision to keep seeing the deeper path of life and committing ourselves to it, in active partnership with guidance.

Life's Companion BY CHRISTINA BALDWIN

Trust has been a big issue of my midlife years, trusting myself, trusting the universe, trusting the herons who appeared in my life during this period without fanfare, so inexplicably, and who have become so important to me. 1995 began with anxiety about new projects and a crowded schedule, including our family trip to Britain and some book promotion time for me. Back in Canada, barely two weeks after I wrote my May entry about trusting, I journaled about the wonderful Meeting for Worship we held in our garden as a part of my 50th birthday celebrations in June.

This birthday lesson in trust took place a week before David and I crossed Lake Champlain by ferry, sharing that memorable heron meditation. Our time of heron communion also turned out to be one day before I found David still in bed, his body so familiar yet so strangely lifeless: he had died in his sleep of a heart attack. Discovering

David dead and coping with all the aftermath of his loss were major tests of how fully I could trust in the Divine net, trust I had a place within it.

Suddenly I found myself a widow: there was a sea-change in my existence. Not only had I been hurled into a new life stage, but I had our seventeen year old son and twenty two year old daughter to try to support emotionally and spiritually. Ironically, David's position as a civil servant in a national museum meant that we were provided for financially, so my money worries were allayed. However, going through his papers revealed more reasons why he had often seemed so withdrawn from me while still alive. For one example, he was having more significant personnel conflicts at the museum than he had ever revealed; for another, he hadn't paid our city taxes in over a year! Yet he had never told me of the colleague issues, the debt, or of his worries. These discoveries were both unfathomable and reassuring — I had thought I knew him better than I did, and I had indeed known communication on many levels was not right between us. His death shocked me — a very final disconnection.

Midway upon the journey of our life
I found myself within a forest dark,
For the straightforward pathway had been lost.

Excerpt from *Inferno Canto 1, The Divine Comedy* by DANTE ALIGHIERI

In those same days of dislocation, I frequently saw herons. They had arrived in my world five years earlier, when I didn't know how much I needed them as the outward sign of the sacred dimension to my life. Established and familiar teachers, during the grieving weeks to come they reminded me to trust I was not alone. In a very cosmic sense, the spiral deepened.

But when I breathe with the birds,
The spirit of wrath becomes the spirit of blessing,
And the dead begin from their dark to sing in my sleep.

Excerpt from *"Journey to the Interior"* in *Collected Poems of Theodore Roethke* by THEODORE ROETHKE

· ·

Friday, 16th June 1995

The fourth night since David died on Tuesday morning. I have done no journal writing whatsoever since every bit of my life flipped, since walking into this bedroom (once ours, now ohmygod mine) and finding David still lying in bed — because he was DEAD ... I prayed involuntarily, "Oh Great Spirit help me ..." AND I saw that in a strange sense, I am free.

Since then, what acutely-in-the-moment days these have been, how many times I have intended to write here, but been interrupted by calls or needs; what surges of grief and anger and loneliness and peace; of disbelief; of wanting everyone with me ... and wishing everyone would just go away.... What thankfulness for these children doing so well, not hiding their grief, and for all these amazing friends, loving us, protecting us from too many calls and visitors, helping us ... And for all the herons.

Sandy came from Toronto and together we found a huge seven day candle to burn for David. Now it glows here, plus other smaller candles for the other losses this one is allied with — for my father and mother, and for my brother and his wife — all premature deaths! ... I'm sleepy, thanks be for that. Just as I was drifting off, somehow I felt David's spirit here, and so I sat up to write ...

In an odd way I've been practicing being a single woman for a long time now; perhaps I can wear this widowhood with less awkwardness.

[For some women] ... a devastating loss breaks into the familiar security of daily life and catapults them into unfathomed depths of their being. In mythology, there are many examples of such descents.... In time, both Persephone and Ianna return to the living, bringing with them the gift of their journeys to the dark realms — a knowledge of vulnerability, of the shadowy parts of themselves and the uncontrollable mystery of death.

The Feminine Face of God by Sherry Ruth Anderson and Patricia Hopkins

I am pumping the pedals of my bike like mad, hurtling westward on the riverside bike path. It's sunset, and the little summer evening gnats are out in full spate, swarming around my head, flying into my eyes which are already full of tears. I swat them away, dab at my eyes, and keep biking, hard. I couldn't stay around any of those well-meaning people in my house any longer, am so heartbrokenly sad and mad ... Furious! Angry! Running away from the sudden stark reality of David's death, from everyone's grief and disbelief, from all that will now have to change. Was it only four days ago? Was he really not quite 53? What a shocking, wrenching upheaval of my life! I pedal through more clouds of gnats, closing my mouth that wants to shout and swear, so I won't eat the insects. Instead, I find I am gritting my teeth, eating rage.

Why him? Why ME?!! It seems so supremely unfair! Why is this world so bloody hard to LIVE in that people go and DIE? How come this man whom I discovered belonged in my life when I was half-way round the world, for heaven's sake, this man with whom I grew and learned for over 27 years, adjusting our two different tempers, cultures, truths, so we could co-exist, raising these perfectly splendid children, how come this good man had to exit early? So precipitously! If there were signals, how come I didn't see them?

I keep pushing westward, keep crying, have passed the big overflow pipe into the river, am heading for somewhere private, maybe for some place where there are herons. I had to get out, get away, hurl myself and my fury at the evening, though I'm too sweaty, and I hate the bugs. Sure, sometimes I hated him, too, hated the quagmires we got stuck in, hated our broken-record behaviour. But I adored him as well, and I was committed to him, to a marriage that could have worked. The sky is past orange now, and the sun's round ball has sunk into striated clouds across the red-tempered waters of the bay. We didn't get to finish solving our midlife problems, and I believed we could have. I didn't get to say goodbye the way I would have liked, no last dance, no last chorus. Big sobs choke up in my throat and are torn away by the rushing air as I bike onwards.

Oh! I brake quickly — there's a heron, flying towards me over the darkening bay, a black shape with those wide, swooping wings that give away its identity. She lands below the path, on the marshy margin which stretches for a few yards between me and the open water, and folds in her wings. Stealthily, she begins stalking forward through black stumps and bushes. I ignore passers-by, hope they will ignore my red eyes which give away my state, and prop the bike on its kickstand.

Blowing my nose quietly, I sit down on the shoulder of the path to watch the heron hunt her dinner. She takes deliberate steps, makes sharp spearing movements: her head jerks up and she swallows a fish. She moves straight ahead, intently focused on food: another jab forward and another flipping, flopping victim is as quickly gone. My fury feels focused, too, stabbing away at my loss, jabbing at why. The universe has swallowed my husband. It seems as cold and slippery a fact as the fish, as harsh a reality as this small dinner drama at dusk.

Soon it will be hard to see — already the heron's shape is blending into her swamp surroundings. If I concentrate, it's possible to track her, to follow her long-legged, continuing search for supper. But is it possible to forget why I am here, or to find any meaning for myself? David is gone. We don't get to continue together, at least not in the tangible ways of human existence. No more sitting down to meals together, holding hands in quiet thankfulness for our food; no more puttering in the garden together, no more putting up with each other, no more nagging, arguing, singing, dancing with David. I don't care if it grows dark around me; tonight the rage inside me is hot and red.

... I can imagine
Pain, turned heron,
Could fly off slowly in a creak of wings.

Excerpt from *"Pruning in Frost"* in *Spacecraft Voyager I: New and Selected Poems* BY ALICE OSWALD

Time's duration measures not the worth of the gift

Which the infinite pours

Into the cupped hands of the transitory.

As long as it lasts

Value it with your whole life....

Grieve not for what lies beyond —

It exists in the heart of the universe,

If not in one form, then in another.

Excerpt from *The Evermoving* BY RABINDRANATH TAGORE

After David's sudden death, I was simultaneously grieving and having significant insights into our marriage and my life. I felt stunned by his unexpected demise and by the way this huge life event stripped away any trivial or unimportant consciousness, and I was immersed in either tears or intense meaningfulness much of the time. And yet I was mostly able to function well when it was needed, to support our almost-grown children and do the practical things that had to be done, to make arrangements, confer and decide.... Then I would stop and be hugged, and weep again.

There seemed little time for journal writing, or for heron-watching, but I remember that in the week after we held our big memorial celebration of David's life, I went back to work for a day in the school where I had been sojourning as a "writer in residence." I had begun to know those students, well enough that they all sent me homemade notes and condolence cards. Given the approaching end of the school year, their teachers and I decided a day of closure would be best, and that I would finish my contract in the fall, with different classes.

Thus, nine days after the death of my partner and co-parent, after this major life shift, I pedalled off on my bike to spend a day at school. I met with both classes, singing some of the songs we had already learned together, discussing their writing. Chris lived nearby, so harboured me at lunchtime, and the day went well — I was in quiet function mode.

But then it was over, and I felt weepy and tired. I travelled home along the bike path, beside the humming traffic of the Ottawa River parkway, blue water in the distance. About a mile or so from home, the path tunnels under the road, and I came up on the river side in dazzling sunlight. I seldom see herons out in the open river, but there they were, a pair of herons winging slowly downstream! They were an astonishing sight, doing their graceful dance around each other, wheeling, rising and sinking as they moved in the direction of the city farther east.

As I stood holding my bike, marvelling at the herons' seeming salute to me, I was further amazed to see one of them turn out, and wing slowly back towards Britannia, the old familiar territory to the west. It was emblematic, an enactment of my own situation somehow. I couldn't help but think of that heron pair as David and myself, of the one that flew in the direction of his beloved museum workplace, as himself, heading on alone into a blue unknown. Meanwhile the one that wheeled west was me, staying here in my own Mud Lake area for now.

I saw the herons separate and continue in their different directions, each strong-winged and purposeful, with a deep awareness of having come to a new stage of my life when I would be single. During that sun-washed time of watching there was no shock, no anger and no grief, just acceptance.

*We grieve all that cannot be spoken, that there is no name for, repeating
for ourselves the names of things which surround what cannot be named.
We say Heron and Loon, Coot and Killdeer, Snipe and Sandpiper, Gull
and Hawk, Eagle and Osprey, Pigeon and Dove, Oriole, Meadowlark,
Sparrow.... All that we say we are saying around that which cannot be
said, cannot be spoken. But in a moment that which is behind naming
makes itself known.... Wood in the table knows clay in the bowl. Air
knows grass knows water knows mud knows beetle knows frost knows
sunlight knows the shape of the earth knows death knows not dying.*

Excerpt from *"Naming"* in *Women and Nature* BY SUSAN GRIFFIN

When David's body was cremated, the ashes were packaged in a simple cardboard box, wrapped in brown paper. A friend who had asked how she could help collected this plain-looking parcel from the crematorium and brought it to our house the evening we held a wake for David, with lots of friends and family gathered to sing and talk and remember him. The next day was to be the formal memorial celebration at the museum where he had worked, and we planned to scatter some of David's ashes in the river flowing by the museum, as a ceremonial coda to the event.

The night of the wake, however, in the bustle of people coming and going, the parcel of his ashes was put down in our bedroom, and if someone happened to tell me it was there, I didn't register the fact. As I went to bed, I found the box and thought for a moment I had overlooked some sort of present brought that crowded evening. Only when I looked closely and read the small label, did it dawn on me that this heavy little package was all that was left, in a physical sense, of my partner. I burst into tears, sought my sister for comfort, and then found myself in a sad fury, kicking that box with great violence, shoving it all around the floor like an obscene hockey puck. Fortunately, my sister understood that I wasn't yet ready to bid farewell to David's cremated remains, and showed no horror or offended propriety.

The next day evolved in such a public way that there was no appropriate time to go to the river's edge with those ashes. Later I broke the parcel open to send some of its dense contents back to England with David's sister. Eventually she made a cairn over them on the mountain top in Wales where we had all hiked earlier that spring, where perhaps David had the first intimation that his heart was badly stressed. Some ten weeks later, after performing at a festival of sea songs on the US East Coast, and after a period of fatigue and undiagnosed illness, David had too literally sung his heart out.

On my desk there is a stone with the word "Amen" on it,

a triangular fragment of stone from a Jewish graveyard destroyed

many generations ago. The other fragments, hundreds upon hundreds,

were scattered helter-skelter, and a great yearning,

a longing without end, fills them all:

first name in search of family name, date of death seeks

dead man's birthplace, son's name wishes to locate

name of father, date of birth seeks reunion with soul

that wishes to rest in peace. And until they have found

one another, they will not find perfect rest.

Only this stone lies calmly on my desk and says "Amen."

Excerpt from *"The Amen Stone"* in *Open Closed Open: Poems* BY YEHUDA AMICHAI
TRANSLATED BY CHANA BLOCH

On July 13th, exactly one month after David's death, our two children and I opened the brown parcel again and took out about two cupfuls of his ashes — heavy and slightly oily-feeling — to keep for our own eventual rituals of remembrance. The rest of the ashes were to be buried at sea during an historic re-enactment of the siege of Louisbourg, in Nova Scotia. Originally, David was to have acted as the shanty-man/musician for a special sailing of tall ships down the St. Lawrence, where all on board would attend the re-enacted siege. Instead, his fellow sailors, many also from the museum world, staged an additional, very genuine, multiple gun salute and sea burial. None of his family or close friends were at Louisbourg for that event, though we helped send off the tall ships with heartfelt speeches and sea-shanties from Kingston, in Ontario. Someone had crafted a beautiful wooden box to hold the original package of ashes; that was as close as David came to having a coffin.

At the museum, a photo of David (which he had chosen for the cover of his recent second recording) has been hung in the hallway where he once had his office, overlooking the river. The museum drama company he started was dedicated to him, and a small brass plaque commemorates his work and leadership. But my singer-actor-director husband has no headstone, no one place for his memorial.

Death is but crossing the world,
As friends do the seas,
They live in one another still ....
For death is no more than a turning
of us over from Time to Eternity.

Some fruits of solitude BY WILLIAM PENN,
Quaker founder of Pennsylvania, printed in 1693

One year later, on the first anniversary of David's death, the children and I walked around Mud Lake and along the Ottawa River, scattering small handfuls of his ashes here and there as we spoke of him. A distant heron or two flew over the lake when we paused at particular places that he had always liked — the high rock overlook, the beaver point, the opening in the bushes near the springs at the north end. Was he with us, was he flying with the herons?

At the nearby rapids on the Ottawa, after watching how the heavier ash particles sank to the river bottom rather than floating away, we three decided — on a sudden impulse — to strip off our clothes and swim. David was always ready to join in with that kind of unpremeditated fun, and it felt as if he was actually encouraging us! The weather was hot and sultry, and our laughing, splashing immersion soothed our bodies as well as our sore spirits. Before we got back to the house again, the wind rose, and shortly afterwards there was a quick thunderstorm.

That storm prevented us from taking one more handful of David's ashes to sprinkle around the base of his favourite potted jade tree. On our return to the house, we found the wind had blown the many-branched jade over on the back deck, and our attention was focussed on righting it, no longer on our relaxed remembering. That night I wrote in my journal, *"The day unfolded in complexity and simplicity: anger, sorrow, peace, confusion, garden, tears and water, including rain on this very book."* [June 13, 1996]

Two more years passed, in fact, before I dug some of David's ashes into the soil of our huge jade. In October, 1998, I moved to my own smaller and more manageable house, and I divided David's last remaining "remains" into three, for myself, my son and my daughter. With my portion, I was pleased to find there was just enough for the jade tree and for a ceremonial spread of ashes around my/our old garden and my new front and back doors. Two loving neighbours helped me say the old ritual words that are so powerful, "Dust to dust, ashes to ashes." Once again I felt David's blessing, his salute to my own going-on. I knew I would sense him in many places as I went forward. However, this account of his ashes has spiralled into a "fast forward," and my story of our more immediate disorientation after David's death continues.

. . . .

Monday night, 26th June 1995

Two weeks since we returned from the Mystic Sea Songs festival in Connecticut on Monday evening the 12th; almost two weeks after that next morning when I confronted David's body. One week ago, last Monday, following his huge memorial event at the museum, I had an amazing high-energy experience there, uncovering many more layers of miscommunication in David's work life. Today, after a disastrous trip to the Old Songs Festival near Albany, I have been at sea emotionally, awash in tears and confusion; exhausted; these sea-changes are too vast ...

My early widowhood was an important time of self-definition. I was beginning to explore truly being on my own, being alone, yet I often ran away from that condition, tried to find people to be with. Two weeks after David's death my daughter and I decided to go to a folk festival near Albany, thinking — mistakenly — it would be good to see many friends (and David's former fans) from that world. We didn't realize how fragile we were, however, and much of the time there we struggled with our feelings. We needed privacy to cry or space to be by ourselves, and instead were surrounded by many good people, all kind, but people in singing and dancing mode, not grieving.

The weekend seemed nightmarish much of the time, and we alternated between trying to attend events and finding places to retreat. Saturday night I enjoyed some of the contra dancing, but came completely unglued at the end of the evening. A young man whose partner I had been earlier asked me to waltz with him for the last dance. Unwittingly, I agreed, and moved into his arms, held out in ballroom position. We stepped out in unison with the music, when suddenly I erupted in heavy tears in the middle of the dance floor! I assured him it was no fault of his, but he was not my David — and ran out of the dance pavilion.

At home again, my grief became more complex. Both anger and longing flared up, even as I progressed spiritually into accepting what was past.

The next month I traveled to a seven-day Quaker Gathering. Midweek, I went out not long after sunrise to join an early morning worship group. We were supposed to meet on the edge of a large pond in the middle of the college campus where the event took place. I planned to jog there, both to get the exercise and to save time. In the misty light I could barely make out the pond which was some distance away, and down a gradual hill. I wondered if I would see any herons in the vicinity, having heard others mention them, and I scanned the sky once or twice.

Running down the path to the pond, gathering speed, I recalled the poem Marge Piercy calls "Morning Athlete," where her "leaden feet ... only infrequently are winged and prancing." I was surprised to exult in how fleet and un-leaden I felt! Then, noticing my long legs stretching beneath my body, I suddenly thought: I am of the heron people. The words completely filled my consciousness and repeated themselves, simple and direct. When I think of this mysterious moment of knowing, I can only say I recognize my heron kinship and feel a basic, satisfying identity.

O make song
for lucid air of morning,
bright blood's beating,
life's flow deep and swift,
a kingdom of joy and awe
for us to dwell in.

Excerpt from *"A Kingdom of Joy and Awe*
by Rabbi Chaim Stern
in *Gates of Prayer: The New Union Prayer Book*

Acutely conscious of missing David as a dance partner and as a life partner, I was astonished when a new friend literally waltzed into my life. It was the last waltz of another contra dance evening, at the Quaker Gathering. I was going to stand at the sidelines, cautious of my heartache, but Robert, a sympathetic acquaintance, asked me to dance. This time I said yes, and he was a wonderful dancer. In no time, we found pleasure in each other's further company, and I discovered that, in the midst of loss and confusion, here was respite, here was someone to balance and swing with! Soon, to my further surprise, this new long-distance friend became my lover, counterbalancing my heartache and loneliness.

Only later would I truly comprehend the important role my body held through all these life changes, feeling my legs as I jogged or danced; finding a welcome new friend and physical partner in Robert; struggling with anger and grief's fatigue, with my sleeplessness and discouragement. That first summer as a fifty year old widow ended with both joy AND two emblematic broken bones: my dismay at their painful reality was another aspect of my healing.

. . . .

25th July 1995

At the K's cottage; Lake Kashebog. About 7:30 a.m. a heron called its slow "Quonk!", so I went out to watch him stalk a misty breakfast — hurrah! The first ever at this cottage! ... Since noting that heron I have reread every journal entry here, from my birthday in June onwards, noting all the gaps and the patterns within these full painful weeks. I keep recalling my cousin's words about being "in deep waters" and "what an abrupt intensity of experience" I am indeed having....

> *Going through any of 10,000 gates we have a direct experience of the sacred.... There isn't any place to find God but in the here and now of [my] own life.*
>
> The Feminine Face of God BY SHERRY RUTH ANDERSON AND PATRICIA HOPKINS

During that summer of 1995 the grieving process, like so many of life's rhythms, waxed and waned. I came to accept those spirals, and was especially grateful for the opportunities many friends and neighbours offered us to be out in the natural world. In late July my son and I spent two days at Lake Kashebog, visiting old friends, with whose young children we both enjoyed playing. Compassionate people, they let us just be ourselves, as we slowly healed from our bruising encounter with death.

The cottage guest room had windows that framed the pine trees and lake to the north, and, on the south side, big sliding doors opened onto a deck that overlooked a swampy inlet. I still wasn't sleeping well, and was grateful for the privacy of this room and for its familiar wilderness view.

Going to bed, I stood and watched the moonlight spread over the water of the inlet, idly wondering if I might see any herons there during this visit where I had — surprisingly — never glimpsed them before. Just at dawn, a loud quonk interrupted my light doze, and I hastened to the doorway in grey morning light to observe a heron hunting breakfast.

While the rest of the household slept on, I turned to my journal, and found I was taking stock of how far I had come, emotionally and spiritually, in the previous weeks. Was my state of shock wearing away? Was I any less confused? What was "normal life" going to be like now, especially when the summer finished and school schedules resumed? Was I ever going to compose anything more than soul-searching journal entries again? As I sat in bed with these questions and my pen, the day began in earnest — not only did the sun rise, but so did the cottage children.

Suddenly I realized the children were calling to me, and I hurried out the lake side of my room to see what the excitement was all about. The answer became a poem — this poem, that I laboured over all that day and the next, glorying in the craft of writing once again, totally absorbed in describing the brief bird epiphany the children and I experienced. By the time the poem was finished and we started home, I knew my love of words and nature was alive and well, despite my scarred spirit. Further, I had learned another lesson about being fully in the present: when I can be so aware of the moment, heartache and confusion fade into the background and are impotent.

OH PAUSE AND HEAR: LOONS NEAR!

So often, when I listen to the loon's melodic moan,
I hear an eerie loneliness,
a throb of once-warm memories,
a cry of homeless sorrow or of long regret.
A loon's solitude seems so cold and deep:
it sobs a lightless, night-time song.

But this day was of a different ilk:
without sadness, the lake as smooth and glassy
as a piece of blue-grey silk,
and the children calling, "Oh come and look!
There's ducks! We never see them!
— And two loons nearby — what luck!"

Their black heads marked a silhouette against the misty sky,
and we slipped into the water to try and follow after.
As we swam so silently, we saw those birds move in,
line up as four — they were a family!
The "ducks" were half-grown young,
their heads just feathering dark.
The parents paddled strongly on, then turned
and called to us (our heads were on their level).

Their strangely merry message seemed to be:
"Oh pause and hear! We're here, you're here!"
And as they called repeatedly, we were close
enough to see their very throats vibrating,
black beaks open, spilling tunes!

Yes, those loons were laughing,
trilling over limpid morning waters!
Some thrilling joy of truly being filled that moment
of aliveness on the stillness of the lake.
Oh glad tidings borne by loons!
Oh fearless present time where pain
and gloom are banished, and life whispers,
"Listen! Notice! Hear! — Loons near!"

15th August 1995 (at Camp NeeKauNis)

Meeting for worship outside on the hill was precious today, as so often here at camp. My sister Betsy sang: "*My life flows on in endless song, above earth's lamentation ...*" and I repeatedly reminded myself to trust the Divine, trust that "Way IS opening", that I have leapt and the net will appear, as the Chinese say. I feel saturated with a kind of grace.... Bless Robert as he starts his journey to visit me; bless my daughter at work in Montreal and my boyo as he leaves camp for a visit with friends in Toronto.

How Can I Keep From Singing

Excerpt from 19th century hymn

My life flows on in end-less song, a - bove earth's la - men - ta - tion...

When Robert told me he was coming to Ontario to a wedding in August, I invited him to visit me at the Quaker camp on Lake Huron that our family has loved for years. To my delight, he saw herons where I had never before seen them, in the marshy waters of Matchedash Bay below the high hill of the camp! Robert gave me important but intangible gifts — gifts of two wonderful companionable canoe trip days which included stories and songs and a number of herons, and also the gift of his support and deep friendship. I wrote in my journal often, frequently rejoicing over him!

18th August 1995

Robert here at camp.... He may be hideously hard to let go of when he leaves on Monday, but my goodness, it is wonderful and delicious, and good for me, to have him here now! Yesterday on our four-heron canoe trip through Matchedash Bay, he told me stories about his tough time at home and school as a boy, because his learning style was so unacceptable then. I feel indignant on his behalf, and am in awe of how gentle he is as an adult after such a rocky beginning. There's a generous quality to him, he's so warmly physical, in ways I didn't know how much I was needing.

21st August 1995

After our last whole day together, and a very late bedtime because we ran out of gas and had to climb the hill from the lake in the dark.... We laughed all the way and went to sleep curled up in each other's arms. I woke there this morning, more relaxed than I have been yet....

. . . .

That relationship was such a sweet surprise, an unanticipated blessing like the herons in my life, off-setting the sad times. Though I wrestled repeatedly with the grief, the rage and the inevitable unanswerable questions that come with sudden loss, I found I had also been given many moments of joy, gifts of the Spirit that seemed to come through this new man in my life. Soon Robert and I decided to make space for our friendship in a way David and I had seldom been able to do in the later years of our marriage. We phoned or e-mailed almost daily, and then every four to six weeks he or I would travel from our distant homes to meet and enjoy each other's company, often going to contra dances together. Our good walks (sometimes seeing herons) and talks, the sheer fun and also the serious times which Robert and I shared over the next eighteen months were truly gifts from his spirit, as well.

. . . .

26th August 1995

[written with my left hand] I fell and fractured my right arm above the wrist on August 23rd, after camp, just when I felt all mellow! Now I have a heavy cast on my arm, and a sling so I can't use my right hand . . . I was talking to Sandy about being angry at David for the ways he closed off so much of himself, kept so many of his thoughts from me. Is this break connected to that? Or to my awareness of how difficult it feels now to ask for more help, feels like I don't deserve any more help? Today a friend at the Penetang Folk Festival said the cast declares I am wounded and different, and must ask for help.

Through the unending act of journal dialogue, questions have become
an intimate conversation with life, with journey, with the sacred....
Life is a great unending opportunity to see things differently, to keep
reframing disaster and discouragement into faith.... We have learned
that we are not alone, and that we have never been alone.

Life's Companion BY CHRISTINA BALDWIN

. . . .

30th August 1995

Bedtime. At home again at last! A week after my accident, and today I got a much lighter weight cast of purple fibreglass on my broken arm. Also rejoiced in two standing herons and one flying, quonking at me, as I stood at the lookout point on Mud Lake. I have been trying to say my *Artist's Way* affirmations out loud every day, the ones I usually write — writing IS possible, but it hurts. It's tricky to remember to say them when I am past my usual early journal hour.

Oh Great Spirit, thy creative abundance surrounds and sustains us....
Nourish me in my faith, that I may add to the beauty, love
and good order of my universe, living creatively and knowing
there is enough resource for all of creation to flourish!

Excerpt from my Artist's Prayer, based on ideas in *The Artist's Way* BY JULIA CAMERON

On my first morning back home I felt very welcome in Mud Lake, sustained by my huge grandfather oak tree and comforted by the herons, even as I wept in impatience for my life to unfold.

31st August 1995

I called Robert late last night, and we had a long talk about "us" which we will continue tonight. This morning, after too little sleep, when I ran with Jessie, I spied two herons fly and quonk, then stand still and fish, plus four small green herons! I also felt clear that I would like to risk the money and relationship issues and go to visit Robert next month in the USA.... I do want the connection to him, and if we continue, I'd expect to invest at least a weekend a month in our friendship. So I am willing to start now, if Robert is....
I treasure all the good things he says to me, from how animated and very alive I am to loving me very much. How he feeds a place in me that was starving!

3rd September 1995

... A fine leisurely morning, and when I went to run and watched the herons' slow graceful wings from the rock overlook, I even sang to them: "*Praise him, praise her, All you lovely creatures — God is love, God is love ...*"

Then I stumbled on the path along the fence and fell down, hearing/feeling something ELSE break [later it was to prove my collar bone]. At first I thought, "Oh good, I'm not nauseous," but then I could tell I might faint, and leaned on the fence and prayed hard, gasping in pain. I think I was praying not to faint, when I came to, with "God is love" repeating over and over in my semi-conscious state. Gradually I realized I was lying on the ground in the poison ivy, and when I got up, very gingerly, saw a neighbour who helped me through his fence gate and home. Another neighbour took me to emergency, and later my son came to pick me up. My daughter was on her way home anyway, so she's here now, and I have talked to many folks on the phone, including Robert, who said he would hold me in the Light. I'm writing all this with my right hand confined in the cast, so it's very spidery... Oh yes, I dreamt of David last night. He was just himself and that was nice, especially as I've felt so little of that kind of presence. In fact, I think I said, "But you're dead," and he reminded me he is planted in my heart.

Praise Him, Praise Her

My variation on hymn *Praise Him, All Ye Little Children.*
Original words anon, tune BY CAREY BONNER

. . . .

7th September 1995

… had a long walk with Chris in the brilliant day yesterday, when we admired a standing heron together. Walked with myself today, watched two far off herons, also standing, and said my affirmations, especially that my body "… is infused with the deep intelligence of the universe…." I am adding the words TRUST and JOY into those affirmations; I've come to think these accidents are just further to all my "fear not" issues….

Despite my broken bones, I am in a very good place, with adequate answers for now. My boyo has his friend Donald staying with us for the year, to be his buddy and help with the drives to and from school, so I am relieved not only of so many hours on the road, but also of many struggles with this growing young man. I have enough money for now and am still living in this place I love, that David loved. Our daughter is doing well, has good support in Montreal.

AND there is Robert, who said last night, "I've been holding you very close to my heart these last few days, could you tell?" Indeed, there are times I completely stop my chattering around/at him, and just feel a wordless contentment that is infinitely precious. So I have my herons, and my prayers, and my growing sense of the Divine, of how cosmically loved I am — yet at that core place I am also blessed by Robert, who holds me in the Light and kisses my little fingers.

. . . .

Of course there were also many times when I longed for David, was discouraged and exhausted. Getting enough sleep was a continual issue, not helped by late phone calls to Robert in the midwest time zone. Another confusion was thinking about David's mum, who had been hospitalized back in England and was not likely to live much longer. I knew I would start work at a series of Artist in Education projects in October and worried whether I could get to her funeral. By mid-September my bones were healing; often my spirits frayed, yet also reknit.

> *Healing does not mean wallowing in or identifying with injury….*
> *It means having the courage to see, acknowledge, grieve,*
> *and repair the holes ourselves (with, if we are fortunate,*
> *loving help from others). It means moving on, patches and all.*
>
> From the essay *"Women's Lives, Women's Stories"* by Jill Mellick
> in *Coming Home to Myself,* co-authored with Marion Woodman

September 1995

Now school has started, my son has a pattern to his days, but I do not. I was inwardly miserable this morning, despite some quiet time reading and journaling. So, I went walking-and-carefully-running down through the conservation area fields to the rapids, then along the road beside Mud Lake, and back up along the west side to the big log where we lace our skates up in winter. Peering out through the greenery there, I saw ducks aplenty, some moving off in alarm. Next I spotted a standing heron who startled, but then settled into a still hunchbacked position. I knelt down to be less visible and held my wounded arms and open palms out across the log, so thankful a heron was there, thankful for the sense of extra support that seeing him, immobile and steady, brought me, in my misery-moving-towards-meaning of this morning. As I said my prayers, a kingfisher streaked across the water between us, an iridescent blue flash of inspiration.

I had been wondering whether there really are fewer herons to be seen this year (late summer usually has an abundance, but not this year), or whether my season of seeing these great birds so often was drawing to a close, but now I was simply glad to be reminded of their meaningfulness for me. When I felt more peaceful and it was time to go on, I rose up slowly. The heron didn't seem to notice, and after I got to my lookout point I saw him again, statue-like, much farther off. I left him, still balanced and attentive, and ran slowly past my old oak tree and back home, feeling still myself, and inwardly well-balanced.

The Good News Bible translation of Psalm 46:10 renders the line *"Be still ..."* as *"Stop fighting ... and know that I am God."*

On hard-to-get-balanced mornings — and there were many after David's death, still are! — I sometimes write lines of questions — and protests! — in my journal, recording the sense of a spiritual response or answer I feel after each. One day, one strong message that I felt was a kind of variation on "Be still and know that I am God." I repeatedly had the impression that I must "lean on" Spirit, asking for and expecting help. Before I finished my quiet time, I turned back to a favourite book, *Life's Companion*, by Christina Baldwin. She affirms that writing about my seeming-too-frequent anguish, my frustration at what I often feel is my too-messy way of being, helps transform those feelings into a sense of balance and blessing in my life.

> *I kept trying to squeeze the journey onto one linear and logical*
>
> *path labeled: straight ahead. But mine was a zigzag path.*
>
> *It didn't want to be contained. Finally, I remembered:*
>
> SPIRIT WORK IS MESSY
>
> *I had known that.*
>
> *But I didn't trust what I knew.*
>
> *Stretching Lessons: The Daring That Starts from Within* BY SUE BENDER

. . . .

11th September 1995

After teaching today, I sat in my friend Chris's kitchen and shed a few exhausted tears, feeling overall desperate to come home and bawl hard. But by the time I got here, I had seen a lovely late sunset heron over on the bay, cried in response and relief, and felt better! Now I need to get to sleep so I can wake up tomorrow in time to e-mail Robert about all that's been going on. Better than calling him this late, I regretfully tell myself and murmur: "All is well."

14th September 1995

Late to bed, and longing to call Robert.... Can't wait to be there at his house, but also scared it may not be as wonderful a time together as at Camp — what if a dozen things are adrift? I just get to trust, and put my tired good heart to bed. May Spirit bless, guide and hold Robert and our relationship. Took my cast off for a shower today!

. . . .

19th September 1995

Still writing in a spidery hand, but flying home happy, after a better-than-even-hoped-for visit with Robert. What a place in my heart he fills, one empty for so long! ... However, I hurt myself a third time today; fell coming out his back door, (bad step, new shoes, rain, rushing ...), and have a really sore backside now. He rubbed it and held me; I shed angry tears around the thought "I don't deserve this extra hurt!" Still, I am wondering if these different wounds are not a profound manifestation of how badly I do hurt, am wounded?

I also think that not only do these "handicaps" force me to ask for human help, perhaps they also serve to remind me to seek Divine help. I have felt very in tune to the Great Mystery while away.... Yesterday a highlight was when we looked down on several soaring vultures from a high cliff above Spirit Lake, reminding me to remember
"Easy does it," as they floated on the updrafts, so at ease....

Late that month I went on a weekend retreat in the Adirondacks with several women, including my friend Chris and sister Betsy; one healer there remarked that *It's no wonder my body is manifesting a few breaks and bruises, because my life is in major re-alignment.*

By October the children and I had weathered the first concert of folk music performed by David's bandmates. We were teary several times, and one particular fiddle tune overwhelmed me with vivd images of waltzing both with David AND Robert! I made a list in my journal of about twenty current concerns or issues to resolve, and wrote, *This is hugely hard right now, living with all this angst and sadness, and with more awareness of questions about house, money, work and the future; feeling too geographically distant from Robert; getting into that cycle of too little sleep and too much worry about all there is to do. Blessedly, my herons are with me lots again....*

I was working in a school in St Catharines in late October when David's mum died, but the message about her passing miscarried. I was unable to go to England, but felt at peace with that outcome. At the end of the school week, Robert flew to meet me and attend a nearby contra dance weekend, as we'd planned; afterwards I wrote about lighting a candle for her, and one for David, and being *... aware of some struggle inside, perhaps beating myself about feeling not good enough, and how that distress is creeping into this gift of a relationship.... Time to sleep, just asking, "Bless me, guide me, hold me."*

Back at home I noted that, *I think the herons said goodbye for the season today. After praying for some sort of 'heron closure' I saw one standing near the road. As I approached the gate out of the conservation area, I saw her rise on those glorious wings and waft slowly off — then heard three quonks!* However, they weren't leaving yet, and continued to sustain me well into the next month.

. . . .

31st October 1995

I am noticing how hard it feels to ask for what I want, how challenging.... It feels like it's not ok for me to ask, that there's not enough resource for me to get what I want attended to.

So is it actually part of our human condition to be close and in contact with others every day? Is that what we are "designed" for? Is this falsely strong, independent Caroline persona (which I project so well) actually being less than fully human? Reminds me of lines I read recently in *When Bad Things Happen to Good People*, "What you do with a tragedy is not explain it or justify it, but survive it, and draw from those around you the strength to want to go on living." So we're meant to lean on others, to hug when we meet, drink tea or share meals and our thoughts; to be all curled up in bed together, telling each other where we hurt, or encouraging one another to be bold seekers....

· ·

Early November 1995

Today was a five or six heron morning, the kind that makes me quietly exultant. It was also a grey, misty, November day, the kind when the coming rain almost oozes out of the cold air before it truly falls. Peering through the mist, I sighted the herons and marvelled at how well these mostly grey birds camouflage themselves among the dead grey-brown grasses and swamp plants.

I watched one heron flying across the lake, and then landing to hunt, with my binoculars; soon I spotted another — and another! — standing near the shore opposite the lookout point. While I observed them, I saw two herons winging low over the area where I had first stopped (so perhaps one of the originals, returned). When I jogged on, I spied one more standing motionless and grey, in grey-black water up to the top of her long legs, near a dead willow tree that was silvery-white in the dull light.

None of these herons were very close, so I was glad for the binoculars, helping define them against their drab swamp ground. The quantity of my grey companions also made me glad, as the natural world feels far from abundant when November settles in, in its sunless way. I myself came home to settle into work, bright-souled.

The spirit of my mother
swooped in the form of a heron
on the shoreline.
She stood at the foot of our
        cabin path,
Flew overhead at twilight.

Excerpt from the poem *"The Spirit of my Mother"* by Jeanette Dunagan
in the collection *Sacred Circle, Writing the Journey* by the Unitarian Fellowship of Kelowna

The old Celts thought of November as the time when the spiritual world came alive, in contrast to the dying plants and falling leaves. For them, this period after what we call Halloween (their New Year's Eve) was a time when all the spirits of those who had died in the past year were abroad. Their new year observances finished after eleven days, on the date which in Christian times became St Martin's Day and then, after the First World War, Armistice Day. Now, in grey November, on what Canadians call Remembrance Day, we officially remember men and women who have died in both the World Wars. My private memories crowd around me, as ghostly as the grey mists of the season.

Perhaps because of my Quaker pacifist heritage, I have little direct sense of wartime losses, and I always think more generally about the members of my family and intimate circle who have died. I am glad to observe a special day that reminds me of all those who have gone on into a realm we only guess at. I have a myriad memories, not just of my parents and grandparents, who all died before I was fully adult, not just of my brother and his wife, whose lives were mysteriously cut off in the Amazon jungle in the 1980s, and not just of my husband David who died so recently. On this formal day to remember, hallowed at least since Celtic times, I also cast my mind widely, recall as many as I can of the great aunts and uncles, of the Ohio cousins and elderly Balderston relations, of dear friends and teachers over the years.

All those who were close to me, but who are now dead, still feel close. As much as the undefinable can be defined, for me these beloved dead comprise a host of invisible companions. They are not so much individual ghosts as a group of spirits melded together, somehow surrounding and supporting me, part of the Divine that I ask to bless and guide me. I pray to remember my connection to this Greater Spirit as much as possible — repeatedly, continuously.

Trying to discern grey herons on a grey day reminds me that we cannot literally see all those who care for us, whether alive or dead, but we can choose to bring them to mind. Similarly, in the broadest sense, our spiritual lives need periods of trying to tune in to the unseen. Quiet times of soul-searching provide a kind of inner magnification, just as the binoculars I use are a tool for seeing the herons better. Oh Great Spirit, may the dull grey days not dismay me.

I am <u>with</u>.

WITH.

And the with is WE:

how many grandfathers, grandmothers,

how many great-aunts,

how many shamans,

how many saints?

With you.

I am with you all days,

even to the ends of the earth.

From the poem for Miss Rumphius in *Out of the Skin, Into the Soul: The Art of Aging*
by Dorothy Albracht Doherty and Mary Colgan McNamara

. . . .

3rd November 1995

I've been at the museum, collecting more of David's things, talking about him and reading his actors' tributes. And a few days ago at a big storytellers' potluck, both David and I were honoured with many kind words about the richness we have shared with that oral community. I felt very attuned to him. The main speaker gave me a smooth driftwood stick, snake and heron-shaped, to underscore his words — I'll treasure it!

16th November 1995

Loads more happening — life goes on at such a pell-mell pace! My final fall Artist in Education week at a school in central Ontario was mixed, but creditable. I drove from there — in early snow! — to Toronto, where there was another memorial concert for David, and came home to new snow falls here....

27th November 1995

Snow!! As I skied to the chiropractor's office this afternoon, with Jessie running alongside, I decided that the very most important thing to be doing in my life is cultivating/keeping my connection to the Divine open — by meditating, journaling, walking in the woods, communing with my grandfather tree there, talking to the chickadees or herons in season, or beavers (Robert and I saw one last week), or the glorious red fox I spotted today out the window. The fox brought to mind my old Toronto neighbour Carol who loved the ways of foxes; she has just died of a nasty lung disease, way too soon, and I couldn't fully say my goodbyes to her.... DAMN these losses!

Then it follows that though we are spirit, we are also these human bodies that die, that suffer, that grow, that ski or enjoy sex or ... So after I do my morning "tune up" with the Divine, it's a matter of how lovingly I live in my relationships and my day-to-day activities. Can I keep those all Spirit-centred? Because that's my goal.

3rd December 1995

I have been storming all week, saying I long to skip this next month, when we are supposed to go back to England to visit David's sister and her family for Christmas and New Year's. It will be good to be with them, as well as painful, I imagine, and I do love them dearly, but part of me just wants to fast forward to January 5th. That's when I will next visit Robert — who seems alluringly safe and loving, though I may be projecting. Still, I am feeling less overwhelmed. At noon today, out on skis again with Jessie in more soft, fresh snow, I was mobbed by chickadees — hungry no doubt, but such a delight! Right away there were two perched on my hand simultaneously, and all told I had at least thirteen tiny visitors. Some may have been repeats, but I'll call it a thirteen chickadee day!

7th December 1995

Too late to be writing, but I want to simply note that I'm feeling pretty terrible, much of the time about what my therapist calls my "wounded child" or the "David Dance". It appears the only way out is through....

The unending paradox is that we do learn through pain.

Walking on Water, Reflections on Faith and Art BY MADELINE L'ENGLE

10th December 1995

Sunday evening — it's been a totally in-tune, blessed day! I do think I've come through some big piece, feel I'm in a different interior place.

At Meeting our hour of worship felt very centred and focused. After someone's message about how "God needs prayer," I spoke about my chickadees as a descent of the Spirit and about working to remember I am/we are always blessed, guided and held.

Later at a holiday concert I was very touched by a Swahili carol and suddenly glimpsed some of those magical Christmas feelings of other years. I thought, "Oh, it is possible I will be happy this Christmas!" Home by evening, tired but grateful my daughter and her main support person are here. How parallel her situation is to me having Robert in my life — we both have lovers helping us through this year. My boyo joined us for a cozy supper by the fire, where the sense of contented family was very palpable.

13th December 1995

St Lucia Day and the six month point after David's death. Rushed … life feels ahead of me; I can't keep up. Not enough sleep and a tight back. BUT I also had a profound realization after Susan Pepper [a friend in my counselling group who lives up the Ottawa Valley], told me how splendid I am, what a role model, etc. I replied, "That's how we are all meant to be, to believe that we are — each one of us — amazing and resplendent and remarkable!" It's like the idea in *The Colour Purple* about God creating purple to enjoy because it gives "him" pleasure. I find it ironic — or lovely? — that "remarkable" was David's word for me, and now is Robert's for me....

I am also thinking about the truth that I have yet to really incorporate, to know viscerally, that things take time, happen slowly, painstakingly if need be, and that IS how life is.

> *There is that of God in everything, what Teilhard calls*
> *'The diaphany of the divine at the heart of matter' itself.*
> *God is immanent as well as transcendent.*

Shaping A Personal Myth to Live By BY JOHN YUNGBLUT

· ·

26th December 1995

[Letter written from England]

Dearest Robert —

It's been a quiet, low-key Christmas holiday with David's family, with tears every now and again. But today was a surprise! We've just come in from a long late December walk along the Thames and through surrounding farmland, with unpredicted sun all day. Despite the cold air, by mid-afternoon the slanting sunlight was warm-looking, and gave a red-gold cast to the landscape.... There were only a few passers-by, and no nearby traffic — all seemed extraordinarily peaceful and beautiful. I felt as if I were in a timeless state of worship much of the afternoon, intensely aware of my surroundings: flashing magpie wings; an English robin cheering us; the bright orange of pyracantha berries gleaming against a brick wall and the glowing golden green of several mistletoe balls, high in a clump of bare-branched oak trees.

Into that quiet wonder came the excitement of a heron on the Thames! We were standing by the river, idly talking and watching the edge-ice glint, the yellow willow branches weeping low over the water, and a number of seagulls afloat out in the middle. Suddenly I saw a bigger bird, with low-sweeping wings, farther upriver, yet flying towards us, and I asked "What's that big bird?" I never thought to see one of "my" herons in England, or at this time of year, but I had barely time to speak before it turned sideways: its silhouette was unmistakable, with that S-curve neck and rounded chest.

Then it spread its wings even wider, to slow down and land, as if back-pedalling with wings, and made a quiet landing just across from us. My sister-in-law said it was a European grey heron — it looked a bit smaller than a great blue — and there it stood, searching for dinner. Someone quoted a funny rhyme to explain:

> *An English heron's grey, not blue;*
>
> *A robin's smaller than with you ...*

There I stood, too, feeling totally, surprisingly, blessed, rejoicing in the day and at this seeming-gift: to see a heron when I was far from home.

Sometimes such moments of heightened awareness seem to arrive just like that heron on the Thames — an unexpected, but totally absorbing and meaningful benison. This English encounter was especially strong, occurring only six months after the enormous shift in my life that came with David's death. For me, part of the joy of such moments is an overwhelming leap of gratitude that follows on from the deep connection I feel. I sing out loud or in my soul, giving thanks. My ability to be of faith, to move forward with a trusting certainty that my life is unfolding as it should, is reinforced by these times.

Over the years I have had a number of heron surprises like that one on the Thames, occurring seemingly out of the blue — and gold! They have always given me pause to think, as well as to be thankful. Heron gifts, truly.

Further After

1995, the pivotal year of my fiftieth birthday and David's death, closed while the children and I visited his and our English family. During that holiday-but-very-tender time, I wrote in my journal about both *"the fragility of these tearful days"* and that I was *"... thinking about a new idea.... What if I come to England to teach for a term or a whole year, [perhaps] in a Friends School? I have no idea how Robert would fit into that kind of scheme, but ... I want to be here for a longer spell than just a holiday; I am so bonded with this family, my friends here, and especially the countryside.... I've suddenly realized I am free to come back, after longing to for so many years."*

One for sorrow, two for joy,
three for a girl, four for a boy.
Five for silver, six for gold;
seven for a secret, never been told.

English nursery rhyme recited whenever one or more magpies is seen.

As we flew home to Ottawa on January 4th, 1996, I journaled about the magpies I had seen just before we left: *A group of five, then a single one. It was less of a sixth, I think, than a reminder of how our sorrow is a big reason for having come to England; actually, I've seen a lot of single, one-for-sorrow magpies on this trip. This morning I felt a very clear sense of saying, peacefully, 'Goodbye, David,' as I ran on past those magical-to-me black-and-white birds.* Then I noted the further sense of a pervasive message *... that I am greatly loved and there is nothing to fear.... 'Keep asking for guidance; keep tuning in, being thankful. All is well. You are loved and guided.'*

Magpies – one's sorrow,
Two's joy.... Time flies, black or white;
My heart flutters wide.

Once back in North America, my relationship with Robert continued in a thirst-quenching pattern of calls, letters and visits. I loved his companionship on so many levels; he was so appreciative of me! Yet we both spoke of our uncertainty about what we wanted for, or were meant to do with, our lives. Neither of us hid our often messy feelings, either. Of course I thought of how different things might have been in my marriage if David and I had been able to be similarly open with one another.

. . . .

9th January 1996

Before I could tell Robert about my day dreams of going to live in England for a while, I had to bawl a bit.... I do hate all the questions in my life these days, hate not knowing what is going to unfold for me, hate having so many decisions to make ... and all that morass of feelings comes along with having a lovely time together!

... We agreed to be committed to this relationship through the [annual Quaker] Gathering in June, no matter how scared or hopeless either of us feels. That's good, and he's good for me!

. . . .

In that new year I worked as an "artist in education" for several weeks in schools in different parts of Ontario, and also began to enjoy a new volunteer role as a board member of the *Friends Journal*, published in Philadelphia. I told heron and chickadee anecdotes there, plus shaped some into formal stories for the Toronto Storytelling Festival in late February, where I was part of a memorial set for David, singing and telling stories alongside our good old friend Sandy.

In March I sat by my snowy grandfather tree near Mud Lake, while little Jessie dog sniffed animal trails nearby, and I wrote out my therapist's sustaining wish for me, *"... that wherever I go, I be whole of soul, and be able to carry with me the tent of being loved, of being always in a state of grace."* And in April I noted I *... was thrilled to see my first herons of 1996 while on a dance weekend in southern Indiana with Robert.... He pointed out the very first of three we saw flying over, so purposefully, as we drove.* Later, walking around Mud Lake and talking with Susan Pepper, my dear heart friend from the Ottawa Valley, *... we* *saw one heron circle above the pines on the west side! ... Oh it was wonderful to see them back! And good to have them all busy about their work, as I must be — after my next nap.*

By late May I wrote of the Blanding turtles basking in the sun near the rock overlook in Mud Lake, *...Shiny buttons on brown logs, and small birds swooping over still sections of water, brilliantly reflected, but no herons — for now! How many times this past winter have I felt strong heron energy anyway, in this very "territory" of water now, but ice and snow then!*

At the June 1996 Friends General Conference Gathering, I roomed with Robert and took a workshop about mask-making and finding our true selves through that process. On the fourth morning, as a part of exploring that session's question, "What is my unique expression of the Divine?" I journaled about the myriad ways in which I both express and seek the Divine, all facets of what I have come to think of as my spiritual journey.

I look at the plaster cast we have made of my face, and at the clay copy, with its closed, blind-seeming eyes, and I wonder if these representations of me are, in fact, very true. These models are so static, whereas I am fluid and energetic; my face is mobile, my eyes light up with laughter or compassion or interest.

Well, I am me — a creative, singing, laughing, crying, long-legged, heron-loving being. I am open, even transparent, and actually don't have much sense of myself as hiding behind a mask, which this workshop leader spoke of. There are many ways in which my life expresses the Divine: I write letters and poetry, I dance, I listen to and affirm those around me, I teach and cook and garden with love, and I commune with herons....

In midlife, I am focused on how those aspects of me, of who I am, have been unfolding. Becoming a widow, a single person again after twenty-seven years of marriage, has brought so many questions into sharp relief. And the herons underscore the process.

Letting go of our fearful and childish
black-and-white simplifications
[good-bad, right-wrong, yes-no]
for the difficult ambiguities of real life
is another of our necessary losses."

Necessary Losses by JUDITH VIORST

· ·

2nd July 1996

Hot July morning, [at the Quaker Gathering] at McMaster. Robert and I finally had a
chance to laugh and cuddle last night, though we stayed awake too late. We do have a
date to explore the heron marshes behind this campus this afternoon, so I hope we have
some more good time together before the Gathering ends, plus get further with all our
burgeoning issues. I am dismayed that despite the joy we have been sharing, we are also
getting tangled up with each other. Those sore places and emotional walls between us
were really overwhelming yesterday when I went to take a shower after midnight, full of
discouragement. How I cried in frustration, standing under the cool water, leaning against the
tiled wall — great tears of giving up, of asking for help because I just didn't know what to do.

It seemed as if my sob-prayers were almost immediately answered with a tangible gift!
When I came back to our room, there Robert slumped, with my long-awaited birthday
present on his lap, saying remorsefully that he'd been so busy he had never had time to
wrap it. I didn't mind that it was late or unwrapped and gladly opened the box. Inside was
a stunning framed picture of twelve small standing herons, delicately cut out of pale blue
paper like a paper doll chain, but arranged in a circle, feet to the centre, each pair beak-to-
beak, on black paper! I felt my heart just melt, instantly forgiving all our difficulties of this
week, though the questions remain, to be explored further. My weary spirit feels so gifted
by this lovely, unexpected creation found for me by this unexpected lover of the last year.
I ask for more help with our difficult places....

· ·

Gradually our togetherness began to fall apart, despite visiting Robert for ten days
later that summer. There were more dances, but additional tangled times. My plans
for an extended stay in England unfolded. Though Robert and I eventually ended our
intimacy, that delicate circle of paper herons in its burled oak frame, hanging in one
of my quiet places at home, is an ongoing gift to my spirit. I also take heart from the
cartoonist-writer Michael Leunig, who affirms that when we pray inwardly, and "... weep
outwardly, this is the breathing of the soul."

I am passionately committed to you, to us, and to our growth in God. I will dance with you, cry with you, laugh with you and pray with you. I know this won't always be easy but, with God's help, I will celebrate with you this gift that we have been given.

Excerpt from the "ceremony of commitment" vows made by two British Friends, in *Quaker Faith and Practice of Britain Yearly Meeting*

· ·

Summer 1996

I am watching a heron both still and not-still, a hunting heron, her sharp eyes alert for a fish or a frog. At first she was standing in pointy-beaked profile, occasionally cocking her head while she surveyed her dinner territory. Then she stretched out her neck until it was almost horizontal, parallel to the water just below, and began to move. She didn't strike, and now appears to be tracking some slow underwater creature, perhaps a turtle....

The shiny lake surface quietly duplicates her long neck and oval feathered body, while her legs glide forward so gradually and smoothly that she seems almost immobile. It's as if she is patiently on guard, besieging this little corner of swamp, in no hurry for her meal. Although she seems to be so passive, making her rounds only inch by slow inch, I know that she is an aggressor, awaiting the time to attack. Soon this act of hunting will come to some sudden, conclusive moment ...there! The heron makes one sharp movement to strike, and her small prey is captured and as quickly swallowed. She resumes her siege, head upright again, still hunting.

Heron, crane and stork are "all solar and water birds that are said to be able to predict the weather. They represent vigilance."

Animal Magick BY D.J. CONWAY

The names of flocks of birds can be so various:
We speak of a flight of doves, a bevy of quail,
a gaggle of geese, or — mysterious! —
a siege of herons. What verbal tales
these groupings hold, such splendid sparks
to curiosity. Here we encounter a nye
of pheasants (who ever knows why?)
— there, rejoice in an exultation of larks!

Verse from my naming poem.

The heron's hunt for food as a stalking, seeking siege reminded me of other uses of the word, and I dug into my files, where I had saved a clipping from "The Islander", from Victoria, B.C. It contained a wonderfully evocative line about "A siege of herons flying home against a sunset sky." Curious as to how many herons make "a siege", I turned to the dictionary. The term comes from time-honoured lists of collective nouns, and a siege in this sense can mean a group or a flock of herons. My Oxford English Dictionary, in fact, says the old lists of companies of beasts or fowls mostly included a "siege of herons," giving a 1452 reference to a "sege of hayrynnys."

However, in contrast to medieval times or the modern west coast of Canada, here in Britannia I have never seen more than a couple of herons flying together at the same time, or seeming to move in some conscious grouping, though my friend Chris did, and some neighbours say they've seen more. But I understand that in the Maritimes numbers of herons often fly together, and I've coveted a friend's print of a large flying heron group — a siege! — on Prince Edward Island.

Still, my experience is usually of single, or serial, herons, and, to me, the thought of a heron's siege bears an implication of a lonely wait. Then there's the idea of being under a military siege, when one group of people endures privations and difficulty while another, besieging, group watches for a way to conquer the first. But the "siege of herons flying home" has none of that connotation — unless they are conquering the sky! I simply note how often I, too, feel under siege during this time of learning how to be un-married, self-yet-Spirit-reliant in new ways. But this simile is only partially appropriate: though stressful, my siege has no besiegers. In fact I have many dear supporters — Robert. Sandy, Chris, Susan Pepper — who are encouraging me!

Besieged by herons,
standing, hunting, winging high,
my soul flies open.

My dictionary also quotes a 1633 author who wrote that "A hearn put forth from her siege ... shall mount so high ..." and goes on to explain that the "station of a heron on the watch for its prey" was originally its "siege", which seems very appropriate to the vigilant heron I observed in Mud Lake. Well, I am on the watch for new paths, new ways to sustain (perhaps "feed") myself. Will I, too, surmount all the challenges of this period of my life? Will I always be besieged with self-questions?

A time-honoured Quaker process is to ask searching queries to help clarify our life purpose and practices, rather than to issue creeds. Can I simply sit with these questions, as I did sit watching the heron, and wait for my next step to evolve?

Do you try to set aside times of quiet for openness to the Holy Spirit?
All of us need to find a way into silence which allows us to deepen our
awareness of the divine and to find the inward source of our strength.

From *Advices and Queries of Canadian Yearly Meeting*

The task, and the joy, of writing for me is that I can play with the metaphors that God has placed in the world and present them to others in a way they will accept.... It is a form of serious play.

The Quotidian Mysteries: Laundry, Liturgy and "Women's Work" BY KATHLEEN NORRIS

One summer evening at dusk, over a year after David's death, an odd heron experience occurred because our dog Jessie was desperate to go out for a walk. In her way she too missed David, who used to take her out for regular nightly excursions. I myself only wanted to go outside to garden, and did that till it was almost dark. Then I hopped on my bike for a quick spin down to the filtration plant, Jessie running alongside.

I biked directly across the flagpole path and the grass beyond it to stand on the north shore of Mud Lake once again, and almost immediately saw three large-winged birds flap up into a central dead tree. Not quite big enough or the right shape for great blues, I thought — perhaps they were black-crowned night herons. A couple of ducks flew across, next a definite great blue heron, quonking, and then maybe one or two of the unidentified birds from the tree followed suit, casually heading into the eastern end of the lake — where their tell-tale droppings reveal many heron roosting places.

Next another big heron flew west, wings catching the wind and light, and a third one soared around the tree area. It was as if they all felt restless and unable to settle, and I felt as if there was something stirring up all these herons! Yet it was also hard to see their shapes clearly enough against the dark trees and in the dim light after sunset, so I wasn't fully sure of what I saw.

Willywite, Willywite, With his long bill.
If he's not gone, He stands there still.

English nursery rhyme

I began to find all the bird movement somehow funny — as if they were teasing me with their raucous voices, their not-quite-visible bodies going in different directions, and their numbers. Here's a heron, there's a heron, maybe that's another one ... no, yes! It reminded me of the first sleepless weeks after David's death, when I felt almost haunted by herons, felt as if I were in a Bosch painting, with long bird beaks boring into me — only this time my situation seemed humorous, not hideous. Driven forth by my dog, even though the evening dusk grew deeper by the minute, I persisted in looking for herons, but couldn't tell what I was seeing! I stood and laughed a bit along with these various big birds, and then said my prayers very gladly, especially as the whole scene seemed like such fun, after feeling quite desperate most of the day, swamped by responsibilities.

Before it was fully dark, I biked on a bit further to the far eastern end of Mud Lake, where the grass goes right to the water's edge, and just as I wheeled close, a great blue, frightened by my arrival, rose up suddenly. In his turn, he wheeled across the sky and trees to the south, and then one other smaller bird-maybe-heron flew back in towards the roosting area.

All in all, I guess I saw six or eight probable-herons, plus just felt lighter, from the laughing, the sense of companionship, seeing so many, so unexpectedly. May we all find time and place to be playful, find companions to share our delight — as Robert has been with me. May we remember to laugh!

Laughter is the beginning of prayer....
[It] can be courage for anyone called
to embark upon an unknown course
along the bitter edge of life.

Beginner's Grace, Bringing Prayer to Life
BY KATE BRAESTRUP

· ·

Hot July noon, 1996

… running along Mud Lake's muddy paths, on my way to swim where the River is deep enough. I spot a heron and stop to gaze. Soon she flies up with such enormous wing movements that I stand, pleased and awed, watching her and the watery reflection of her wingspread. She floats low over the water surface and button bush scrub, seeming a bit aimless. Finally she settles a bit farther off, her meandering over, folds her wings, and quonks at me gently.

Not only does that unique sound somehow feel companionable, but I am uplifted to see the beautiful twinning of her wing movements and their reflected image. I haven't seen

this special kind of heron flight for a long time, and it's just what I need, reminding me to make the next moves in my life and be full of faith that they will be matched.

The heron reminder is synchronistic, as well — I spent the morning trying to sort out many logistical decisions. For a while now I have been wanting to spend time in England. So I have boldly decided to postpone using my grant money from the Regional Arts Council here, in order to subsidize a research and writing trip to Oxfordshire next year. After all these years of being in a family, I will live by myself in a rented cottage, for three months of gentle English spring. I also want to investigate the possibility of a further trip, the following year, to teach in a Friends School there. Will I be all right? Can I afford it? How will the children manage without me? Who will care for Jessie? What about Robert? Will it all work out?

Just when all there is to arrange and take care of threatens to overwhelm me, today I recognize that reflected heron image and feel gifted, encouraged. It helps to see the lovely heron metaphor again, to reaffirm that if I do my part, if each of us does our part, surely we will be met.

Later on, driving beside the river en route to do errands, I spy several standing herons. Each grey erect body is far off, though I can also see that each one is preening and turning. As the herons turn, each white-barred head catches the light. I turn towards my own next tasks, renewed, and call out to Spirit: may this glad confidence stay with me; may I also repeatedly catch and reflect the Light!

Autobiographical philosophy ... moves in a spiral direction, circling around and around the great mythic questions. The spiral journey may be the best metaphor for the spiritual life because we seem to discover what we have always known and forgotten.

Hymns to an Unknown God BY SAM KEEN

- -

July 1996

A splendid morning outing today, swinging west on my new roller blades, seeing how far little dog Jessie and I could manage to go along the bike path, hoping I might see herons. See them I did indeed: probably four different birds, but six distinct sightings! A momentous six heron day, whereas some days along that path I don't see any.

The first heron — a tall grey fellow standing and stalking his dinner — was just beyond the overlook where a big drainage pipe empties into the river. I spotted him and kept rolling, but then decided to stop and say my prayers, so circled back. Looking across the August spread of purple loosestrife at that heron, I whispered, "May the radiant light and the healing energy of the universal love be active in this place.... "

The heron waded methodically through fairly deep water, stopping here or there, occasionally spearing a fish, sometimes turning a sharp-billed silhouette towards me, sometimes less visible. This business-like, stay-at-home-heron was exactly the right message for me today, as I too had chosen to work at home and had plenty to do.

Thankful for the focussed quiet time spent with that heron and the beautiful day, I called Jessie and pushed off, on westward. Soon there was another heron standing on the purple margin of the blue river; then I caught sight of yet another. Farther along, where the path runs through a large park, there was one more, wading in the river's edge pool where I frequently see herons. Today there were too many people for me to stay and commune, so we started back, and I glimpsed two more watchful herons en route.

Whatever their number, all of today's great blue herons were standing or wading, none flying; all of them seemed busy about their business. And so I go about mine, asking for focus like the herons, reciting a line I often use, shaped while absorbed in *The Artist's Way*: "... My dreams come from God, whose one thousand unseen helping hands are ever with me, with us all, longing to midwife them...." For me the herons are a part of those God-given helping hands.

> *In my experience, the universe falls in with worthy plans....*
> *[It] is prodigal in it support.... Some of the helping hands may be*
> *something more than human.... Take a small step in the direction*
> *of a dream and watch the synchronous doors fly open.*
>
> *The Artist's Way* BY JULIA CAMERON

• •

Late August, 1996

An end-of-summer day, back from visiting Robert.... Running north along Mud Lake, I paused to look around near the underwater springs. I often wonder whether I will see a heron at that end, but haven't all year, so was surprised to spot a heron standing not far off, vigilant and tall. Rejoicing, I watched him and began to repeat my prayers, "As I listen to the Creator Within, I am led, balanced and blessed.... "

However, he wasn't staying, and lifted off with that familiar broad wing motion, one push and then a second to be airborne. His rich blue-grey reflection clear below him, he flew out across the lake, quonking as he departed. I felt more that he was scolding me for disturbing him, rather than giving me any messages, today. My mind kept turning over some anxious questions, "Will Robert stay partnered with me, will our lives continue to reflect one another?" How confusing to be still mourning David yet wondering about Robert's place in my life.

Still, I was glad to see that heron, and watched his flight path to my right till I couldn't discern him any longer. Then I heard a quonk again, and saw him flying out across the lake, followed by a second grey drifter, who also called out. They circled around, till I could barely see them without binoculars.

A few minutes later, scanning the lake once more from the north end, I saw one of these two great fellows stretch his wings and fly up and around the beaver lodge. He hesitated, then decided not to resettle, and set out across the middle of the lake, heading towards the dark pine trees on the west side. He veered in towards a roosting place, but didn't stop, just slowly circled around and then flew all the way back across the water, not so slow as sometimes, but deliberate and rhythmic, allowing me to watch for quite a long spell. Appreciating his sky-flying silhouette, I sang to myself,

> *Wearing my long white feathers as I fly,*
> *Wearing my long white feathers as I fly,*
> *I circle around, I circle around,*
> *the boundaries of the earth.*
> *The boundless universe ...*

Today was feeling like a hard day, full of many urgent tasks, at the same time as I felt my sore heart was numb, my awareness of the Divine hidden and my healing not easy to track. But now it's all less so. These herons in flight, plying their wings with such regular, sure rhythm, aiming for their own goals, alighting where they choose, moving on when they are ready, seem purposeful. I ask to be as purposeful, giving thanks for at least a three-heron-day!

. . . .

There are moments in our lives, there are moments in a day, when we seem to see beyond the usual — become clairvoyant. We reach then into reality. Such are the moments of our greatest happiness. Such are the moments of our greatest vision.... At such times there is a song going on within us, a song to which we listen. It fills us with surprise. We marvel at it.... We live in the memory of these songs. They are the pinnacles of our experience and it is the desire to express these intimate sensations, this song from within, which motivates the masters of all art.

The Art Spirit BY ROBERT HENRI

Early September, 1996

Just at dusk, hurrying home on my bike, speeding along a path around the eastern end of Mud Lake. I can only dimly see, but despite the encroaching dark, the being late and feeling chilly, I cannot pass the open water; am irresistibly pulled to stop. Oh! Is that a long-necked grey bird, out in this swampy corner of the lake?

The bird's body is the shape of a Canada goose, I think, and its head is about the right size, on a periscope neck, but does it have more grey than black feathers? Whatever, I am fairly sure this bird is moving its neck with the forward-and-back rhythm that characterizes herons, not geese. And yet it seems to be up to its feathered belly in the water, and going fast, as if it is swimming — but herons don't swim! Plus, in the fast-fading light I can't make out if it is really grey. Seeing what is truly there is often like this — we are unsure, perhaps confused by other factors in a situation which may colour our view or blind us to what spreads before us.

Two other large birds, likely night herons by their shape, wing across the water, distracting me from my puzzled vigil for a minute. Are they roosting on that dark tree, I wonder? Then loud splashing sounds near the bird-heron-goose I was originally watching draw my attention back to that section of the water. Broad, flapping wings and the awkwardly wheeling body of a heron as it rises up, confirm my guess at what I was seeing. The light is too faint to be sure, but it looks like the heron had been intently following some creature for supper, and then in the process of catching it, lost his balance, maybe even his meal. He flies off into dim, disguising brush, wings wet, possibly hungry, perhaps a bit disgusted to have been witnessed in such an undignified struggle, and I bike off home, chuckling. What a story I have to tell Robert!

Somewhere in the darkness the arc of the night heron's stride

Anonymous haiku in *Heron Dance*, #24

Spiritual growth demands an openness to experience and a willingness to accept the challenge of self-knowledge despite the suffering, confusion and agony of spirit which this can involve.

From the foreword BY BRIAN THORNE *in Telling Our Stories* BY ALISON LEONARD

Herons are usually so deliberate in their movements, and graceful, rather than gawky — it was so atypical to see that heron in a commotion! However, once before I caught sight of another silly looking heron making what seemed to be a mistake, on the St. Lawrence. He was stalking along the margin of the river just a short distance away, but all I could clearly see were his neck and head above the edge of the grass where I sat.

In any case, that heron moved along his hidden pathway very purposefully, his neck and head rhythmically bobbing along, forward-and-back. All of a sudden, he made a quick spearing movement downward: I just glimpsed his beak flash and his neck bend. For a second I couldn't see heron at all, and then there was an almighty squawk and furious beating of wings. I stood up to watch this river's edge rumpus more closely. The formerly deliberate heron seemed to start up the bank and then completely lose his footing, becoming a tangle of wings and beak, grey body and edge weeds.

I had the impression that something intended for food had escaped or even attacked, seriously ruffling the feathered dignity of that stalking heron. I found myself observing this gawky heron with a grin; he flew off quickly, in some disarray, as if in a huff, quite discomfited. Was there also an irritated final quonk? I can't recall.

Now I don't suppose that birds really feel embarrassed. Nor do our dogs and cats or caged birds probably register all the feelings we attribute to them. And yet, as with our pets, somehow these herons in their different, even humorous, struggles reflect back to me an awareness of other realities. I remember talking this over with Susan Pepper, saying they give me — what? — perspective? In addition, knowing these usually careful, controlled creatures not only make mistakes and miss their dinners, but can make a mess of themselves as well, helps me to smile at myself and my own mistakes and messes. May I ever be open to the ability to grin, to be awkward and unsure.

. . . .

Mid-September 1996

I run to the edge of Mud Lake where the large bare log makes a good seat, and find the opening is blocked by a big maple sapling. The beavers have chewed it down — they perennially resume activity as autumn settles in. I heave and pull the sapling into the water (where I hope the beavers will claim their rightful booty), which scares a lot of bird life. Dozens of migrating ducks fly up, quacking and fussing, and a number of grebes are frightened away. Far off two herons move on down into the swamp, their wings startling white in a sudden gleam of sun between grey clouds.

I stand and watch the ducks flap out of the water, awkward and noisy in contrast to the great blues' silent rising; the ducks' wing movements actually whistle — in a rusty, inefficient-sounding way — as they go. Herons, in comparison, seem so deliberate and slow, so sure. It's as if they decide to move on merely because their human observers are being inconsiderate. They may fly off, but prudently, never in a panic like the ducks literally "in a flap." Despite their size, those great grey wings are hushed, and when the herons quonk at me, they may seem annoyed in a superior way, but not to scold out of fear, like their smaller feathered fellows.

The Great Blue Heron
spreads his grace-filled
wings in a meditative flight,
having never known
the need to rush, all he ever
needed is within his reach.

Excerpt from *"The Great Silence"* BY PATRICIA G. ROURKE in *Friends Journal*, August 1998

It's true that herons usually seem quite fearless to me, whether standing their watery ground or wisely departing when conditions are not good for them. And this I ask for myself, for all of us: fearlessness. Further, I ask for the wisdom to know when it is a moment to be still and stay where we are, remembering our deep connection to the Divine, or when it is time to move on.

To decide to change a situation, decide something is not right, and to declare it as clearly as the heron quonks, is a radical act. As a child I did not have these wise models and actually learned an opposite sort of behaviour. A young girl in a large, judgemental family, I adapted an accommodating, equivocal pattern, trying to please, or at least to second-guess, everyone around me. No longer a child, I have grown to see that I can choose a different stance. No longer even a wife, I am relearning how to be centred in self, realizing that it is different from being self-centred. David and I struggled with our needs for autonomy and fulfillment within our marriage, and in several ways he opted out. Enter Robert and the joys we've shared! He and I have been trying to navigate similar paths, though we haven't made long-term promises to one another.

At mid-life, the herons call to me to leave behind old accommodating ways and proudly fly my own course. May I decide for myself where to stand or settle.

When I allow myself to become fearful, I disconnect from God.

Tom Fox, Quaker member of the Christian Peacemakers Team killed in Iraq, 2006

. . . .

November 1996

Grey air, grey water, dark weed stalks and tree branches, grey day. Nothing is clear, nothing fully manifest. Hard not to be grey in spirit, as well. As I ran round the fog bound lake today, I wondered if I saw the dim shape of a hunched heron, out among some rotting stumps. I stood still to observe more closely and began to say my prayers, then realized it didn't matter whether I was seeing a heron or not, as long as I remembered my connection to Spirit, remembered to take the broad view and to still myself.

I will affirm my heron connection to Spirit today, and also my goal of clear focus even as I go busily to and fro. My old friend Sandy called and shared some deep wisdom with me a few nights ago, about aiming for clarity and continually checking to make ourselves clear channels for Spirit to work through. She believes this is what being human-in-these-physical-bodies is about, that our task is to make Spirit manifest.

Having thought I had seen the end of manifest herons for this season, last week I did see two more on Mud Lake, one standing motionless on the beaver lodge and another flying up from near the shore path by the springs, quite unexpectedly. I watched those great wings take the second heron out across the ruffled water and was thankful for both images, the one which suggested standing-still-in-God, and the other moving-purposefully-with-the-Spirit.

I start my paintings by covering the surface
in grey — grey is neither light nor dark.
There is no separation of colour. Everything comes out of grey.
A place of no separation, no judgement, no duality.
From there, I paint vague images.
Out of the grey emerges light and dark. White and black.

NANCY DEAN MERCURY in *Heron Dance, #21*

A duck riding the ocean a hundred feet beyond the surf...

He sits down in it.
He reposes in it as if it were infinity —

which it is.
That is religion, and the duck has it.
He has made himself a part of the boundless, by easing himself
into it just where it touches him.

Excerpt from *"The Little Duck"* BY DONALD C. BABCOCK

Just how DO I make Spirit manifest when I am not out where I can see herons or breathe in the wide view? This is exactly the challenge. Sandy's wise counsel to keep checking that I feel clear does help, yet sometimes I forget — at precisely the point when I need to centre down! May my memories of herons help Spirit shine through my words and actions, wherever I may be.

[A woman must be willing] to cultivate the sacred in her life. It is not tools or visions but the repeated conscious use of those tools that lets our seeds bear fruit. This perseverance is perhaps the hardest part of cultivation....

The Feminine Face of God BY SHERRY RUTH ANDERSON AND PATRICIA HOPKINS

One early spring Saturday I travelled up the Ottawa valley to a healing workshop led by a wise woman: it was a day full of her gentle touch and many insights. The group followed her guidance to envision a "symbol of attunement," a scene or image to help in centring down. I vividly recalled herons flying over me during the summertime, when I do tai chi on the beach just at dusk, and so my symbol became that of a heron flying purposefully, with powerful wide wings.

That image is strong! Can i bring it to mind when I get lost in grief or confusion, get frazzled or frantic? Then I can use it to remind myself of my relationship to Spirit — that "it" is always flying over and around me, if I but remember.

Of course when I am calm, I CAN remember Spirit, can recollect previous moments of wisdom and understanding or inspiration. But I also know that if I am rushed or self-critical, it's much harder to recall my connection to the deeper places. Or, if I am overworked or tired, I may forget what I have found before, and can re-find: a sense of being in tune to Spirit — and myself. This means confronting my core issues again and again — oh, the spiral aspect of life! — but this time I have a new tool to help, thanks to this healing symbol of attunement.

The workshop day also included my first heron of the year, flying far overhead, winging steadily upriver in the evening sunlight. Our host and I had gone for a companionable walk along her part of the Ottawa, near Constance Bay, examining the breakup of the ice, when suddenly I spotted that high, early heron — how I rejoiced at the synchronicity! Very soon I, too, would be flying, flying off to England, to live by myself, write, read and research for many weeks. It may be that I will feel alone in a chilly world, without easy calls to Robert, without even my little dog for company, may well need to remember this symbol.

The challenge now is to live with this paradox: to hold onto my heron symbols, to tune in to them in moments of stress, and simultaneously, to forgive my very human fallibility. As life spirals onwards, I trust that there will be new symbols of attunement, or that a former precious one will be revitalized and take on fresh meaning. O heron of the purposeful, over-arching flight, help me remember we are held and guided by Spirit.

"... The great blue heron for me has become a truly religious symbol ... [of] the connection I felt between sky and lake, creation and created, life around and life within, [giving] me a sense of companionship, a link with the life forces....

JIM LENHART in Quaker Universalist Fellowship newsletter

One of my most repeated prayers is simply to ask Spirit to "Bless me, guide me, and hold me (or someone else)." Sometimes, rather than a petition, the words shift to a thanksgiving. I can see how well my life is unfolding, and I actively feel blessed, guided and held. These words came to me in a time of guided meditation, not long after David's death, and since then I have found myself asking and being grateful for blessing, guidance and a sense of being held by Spirit — often many times each day.

I used this prayer intensely before my first spring sojourn in England. How I leaned on those prayerful words throughout the very hectic time of tying up the loose ends of my life at home in Ottawa. Finally I was settled in my temporary Cotswold village home — and my prayer evolved! Going for a sunset walk, I passed the parish church notice board and realized it was almost time for evensong. I felt in need of some worship, still a bit off balance by all the rushed preparation for my sojourn, so decided to join the tiny congregation sitting in the choir stalls section of the old stone nave. As I settled into quiet prayerfulness before the formal service began, I was tearfully yet joyfully conscious of an inner asking, as so often, to be "blessed, guided and held," yes — but also of a new request, for Spirit to "use me". There I was, in an Anglican church, not taking communion, not even reading the set prayers, but deeply in touch with Spirit in my own way.

Further, I was aware on some deep level of my own spiritual growth. Almost two years had passed since David's death precipitated so many changes — including this extended trip to England, where we had begun our married life. After the long period of grieving, raging at and healing from my loss, I was ready to be more of service to others, to look outside myself for ways in which Spirit could use my hands, my voice, my prayers. My worship was filled with a sense of Divine presence, and of gratitude. Frequently now my words extend to "… and use me for the good."

The next morning, when I set out on my "Cotswold" bike to do some errands, I found myself shouting my prayer line to the sky — surprised by a large grey bird. Above the hill opposite my English driveway, where I never expected to see a heron, I saw that slow-flying, unmistakable shape. I had had no idea there might be herons in the Cotswolds. Without conscious thought, I called out a jubilant "Bless me, guide me, hold me — and use me!" — both as thanks for the end of my trans-Atlantic journey and safe arrival, and as invocation for the weeks to come.

God within me, God without,
How shall I ever be in doubt?
There is no place where I may go
And not there see God's face, not know
I am God's vision and God's ears.
So through the harvest of my years
I am the Sower and the Sown,
God's Self unfolding and God's own.

"Invocation" attributed to ASMUND KARASUN, ca A.D. 1050

In the summer of 1994, a year before David's death, I had journaled:

There was a standing heron near what I call Heron Point on Mud Lake this July morning, and later during a Quaker committee meeting out at Sharbot Lake, I saw two herons flying far off — both made me think, "Fear not, for lo I am with you always ..." Afterwards I asked if anyone could tell me the full Biblical quote or reference. I went for a nap saying this phrase to myself, hugging a mental image of birdly comfort.

I woke very refreshed, and that energized feeling of being tuned in to Spirit continued after supper as we walked to the lake, and later drove home. It was almost as if I were wrapped in Spirit in a very "gathered," or deep Quaker Meeting for Worship. Such a strong sense of "I am with you always" enveloped me in the car that after a bit I began to wonder if some big loss or harm might be coming — strangely, I thought of David. But as we travelled along a very desolate section of highway, and I scoured the bush swamps which usually seem uninhabited to my eyes, I saw another standing heron. Its quiet beauty not only gave me pleasure, but an additional sense of having nothing to fear!

I want to remember, constantly, always, this awareness of God-with-me and the need to fear not, as the Bible enjoins. To help myself with this faith that seems so hard to hold to, I will watch for all those "unseen helping hands" which Julia

Cameron praises and I am learning to invoke, especially watching for what appear to me to be helpful bird messengers.

Further, I want to remember that my heron sightings (and sometimes feeding the little chickadees) are times which help me feel deeply connected both to my soul and to a larger Spirit. The herons and chickadees seem almost eager to remind me how precious and unique I *am*, life IS ... that there is purpose and meaning to my existence. When I forget, these repeated moments of bird blessing help me re-focus.

There was a painful irony in finding this old journal entry some time after David died. Our awareness works on so many different levels! By the time I read over these lines, I had begun to look at my changed status in terms of its several opportunities for growth. My new situation had catapulted me into far greater self-responsibility and, simultaneously, an increased trust in the Divine. I knew I was enormously sad, and angry, but also loved by so many, and I generally did not feel afraid. Everywhere I turned there were helping hands for the practical problems, and sometimes there were Robert's arms to hold me for dancing or cuddling. On a spiritual level I often felt more held and protected than ever before. In addition, I rejoiced in heron sightings that continued to add layers of meaning to my life.

Later, during my 1997 spring in England, I discovered another bird messenger....

I stood under a shrubby tree on the way home from a good afternoon walk by myself today, and just listened, in a fully attentive, full-souled way, to a cheerful robin, warbling away right above my head. I was so close I could see his feathered throat throbbing, and his tiny beak open, and it seemed to me that his message was to be of good faith. Well, I promised him, and myself, and the Great Spirit, that I would rest in that good, deep understanding.

I am bemused to learn this lesson from a little robin in this land of no chickadees, where I seldom see herons. So I note that the English robin has become yet another bird teacher or messenger for me, bless him back for blessing me, and affirm I will be unafraid!

Months later, in an exhibition called "Beadwork in Iroquois Life" I learned that birds are important in the Iroquois creation story, symbolizing spiritual and physical strength. In their legend, the chickadee gave its life to decide the fate of the world, and in their beautiful traditional beadwork, the Iroquois often show birds with berries hanging from their beaks, signifying gratitude for the abundance of the world.

Your power ally is a certain species with which you have recognized
an important connection. This species becomes your teacher,
with whom you allow yourself to grow and learn. Nothing can replace
the observation of these creatures in their natural habitats,
for this connects you with the Earth, the animal and the Great Mystery.

Medicine Cards, The Discovery of Power through the Ways of Animals
BY JAMIE SANDS AND DAVID CARSON

. . . .

Early May 1997

Writing on the train, after visiting old, good friends in Yorkshire.... Although I will return
to teach next year, this England trip will be over soon. This morning I had a moment of
profoundly recognizing that it's also time to go. I went out for a jog and really enjoyed
running up a little road called Blossom's Lane into the country, then back into the village.
I turned down a footpath that came out onto a wooden bridge which I remembered I had
been to years ago, crossing a millpond aflutter with ducklings. Then, meeting the ubiquitous
dog-walker, I thought of Jessie in Ottawa with her caregiver and told myself I'd see her soon!

Next I ran down towards the old church, and came upon an unfamiliar place, beside a little
swampy lake which seemed a likely area for herons. I clambered around to get closer to the
water, and although there was that "feel of herons" I often get, couldn't spot any. Then I
started thinking about how at home, by this time, all the herons would have migrated back
to us. Suddenly I got such a strong sense of communion with "my" herons! I thought of my
dear dog-walking companion Chris, wondered whether she and her dog would have been
out to Mud Lake recently, and whether she was watching herons. I burst into surprising tears
as I realized it IS time for me to go home, accepted that this sojourn is indeed about to be
over. I feel more ready to go, more willing. This has been a blessed period, and I look forward
to returning to England, but now it's time.... I feel peaceful, pray that all the things that
remain to do won't be too overwhelming, trust I will hear from Robert soon.

I'm staring out the windows of the train as I write, noticing lots of potential heron waters — marshes and ponds, rivers and canals. We are crossing the Humber River and the surrounding farm lands are very green and very flat, all rainy-misty: the same weather and landscape I remember from my Yorkshire years of early married life with David. Oh hurrah! I just glimpsed a standing heron, clear as clear, in a canal beside the train.... Such a fleeting moment, yet it confirms my heron connection today.

Poetry is an exercise in patience
You must wait for it to come to you.
The spirit manifests in many guises,
Some quiver with beauty,
Some vibrate with song.
What is happening?
Slow down, slow down,
take a few deep breaths,
read the poem slowly,
read the lines one at a time,
read the words one by one
read the spaces between the words,
get sleepy, this is poetry,
relax until your heart
is vulnerable, wide open.

Excerpt from *"You are reading this too fast"* in *Whirwinds* BY KEN NORRIS

Looking back, my awareness of herons was heightened all that day and the next, when I had a marvellous chance to tell some of my heron and other bird stories aloud to a lovely all-ages Quaker audience. I had told some of those anecdotes before, but never so fully or to such a receptive group. It felt magical, as if I were invoking the spirit of the English herons and those at home, to sustain my telling.

That sense of being called home which I was given in Yorkshire stayed with me throughout my final period of packing and farewells, of travel and transition. It was as if I were well supported by, and had received some strong energy from, the images of my herons. My internal awareness of these birds which are so special to me seemed so real. Who can say, in the end, what is real and what is not?

When my son was little he used to be fascinated by the idea of where a thing starts. He would pelt us with questions about where all the vehicles go when we can't see them, or where did the line of traffic "begin." He grasped the strange truth that although he did see many cars and trucks around us, there were far more before and behind us — and he always wanted to be able to pinpoint the theoretical "first" one.

It stretches us to understand that cars are moving in many corners of the city, let alone of the world, but we can't see or hear them. Indeed, it's challenging to truly know that people are being born and dying constantly in places we can't see, even as we read these words, as we live out our own small dramas in our particular corners of the earth. And so with the herons, here and not-here. How much can surround us without being tangible!

. . . .

13th June 1997

[back in Ottawa] On the second anniversary of D's death, I returned from taking our dog Jessie for a hasty walk, hurrying to meet both children arriving from Toronto. (We had plans to observe the point of two years passed together). I was feeling a mixture of anger, sadness, and worry, wishing I had seen herons in Mud Lake, trying to hold onto what I remembered of my connection to them, through them to Spirit. In such a state I came up the steps into the main part of the garden and there, in a straight line across my path, was a long, beautiful snake skin!

Despite my heavy gloom, I saw that skin as a wonderful spiritual sign post: that I am, bottom line, shedding my own old skins, and in the midst of transformation.

Remember, love would not have carried you this far
to let you down.... Trust on and move on....
Keep going into the unknowing....

This Time I Dance BY TAMA KIEVES

Why an almost translucent, paper thin snake skin spoke to me that anniversary day, instead of herons, I cannot say, only that it was a powerful moment of recognition, of confirmation that I am evolving, am changing, will emerge in my own new skin, even though it often feels otherwise.

On the summer solstice, a week later, I nearly stepped on a similar skin, stretched right across a water's edge rock. I had been swimming with a group of women friends, gathered to support each other's growth. That second straight line of snake skin again gave emphasis to my reality, that I am at work on myself and my life, in a time of transition. I loved realizing all this on this special sun day, not a very significant date in our society, but full of meaning for me.

Not long after, while cleaning the garage for some physical respite from my mental work of wrestling with words, I found two more snake skins in the woodpile. In fact, I have repeatedly found bits of snake skin there since David's death — the rough bark of the logs must give my garden snakes an ideal place to slough off their old coverings. This pair of dry papery skins were unusually whole, however, each about two hand spans long, complete with the head and eye holes.

Such emblematic discoveries as these cast off, yet quite intact, skins astonish me. Of course I cannot claim they were literally put in the woodpile or left in my path for me, any more than I might assert that herons rise up from Mud Lake on my specific behalf. And yet, and yet … I am receptive to them, ready to learn some life lesson that these snake skins, these herons, somehow help me understand. Amazing — transformation, indeed!

Each journey has its gifts. Not all of the gifts are welcome but each does, indeed, carry the potential for quiet transformation.

From the essay "Women's Lives, Women's Stories" BY JILL MELLICK
in *Coming Home to Myself* CO-AUTHORED BY MARION WOODMAN

• •

July 1997

A new resolve — part of being back, part of my changing life! I am determined to start my daily writing work with a prayer, with the acts of centring, giving thanks, and making a request for blessing and guidance each time I sit at my desk. In 1993 asking for help was a wonderful way to begin work on the last high-pressure stages of *Eleanora's Diary*, as I progressed each day. Today I promised myself I will record this resolution for this new manuscript of heron reflections, this awareness-becoming-words-to-share, this next book which "is a-borning." That was the phrase my dear upriver friend Susan Pepper used in a letter she sent while I was in England. How unutterably sad that she cheered on my book's birth, but would not live to see it. I am grieving her death and yet committed to move forward with this creative writing challenge.

I made this fresh decision to pray for my work while I paused on the shore of Mud Lake, going over my morning prayers, which have grown increasingly meaningful since I began crafting them through my *Artist's Way* work. This time I spoke them aloud to the listening lake, and it felt as if Susan were listening, too. Her spirit was there, with the wood ducks (plenty of them today), with the loon (I am pretty sure I saw one, surprising though that is here), and with the sense-of-herons all around me.

When despair for the world grows in me

and I wake in the night at the least sound

in fear of what my life and my children's lives may be,

I go and lie down where the wood drake rests

in his beauty on the water, and the great heron feeds.

I come into the peace of wild things

who do not take their lives with forethought of grief.

Excerpt from *"The Peace of Wild Things"*
in *The Collected Poems of Wendell Berry* BY WENDELL BERRY

Susan's suicide was a sudden searing shock. I storm at whatever despair precipitated her act! I remember her bright eyes and warm friendship, and I look hard at the paradox of being and not-being. I think this means I must embrace the seeming contradiction that this gutsy woman who understood the birthing of a creative project and extended her support for mine to me, she who was so very alive in this finite world, somehow opted to end her human life. Susan, who had given birth three times and who knew the infinite cycle of seasonal rebirth, somehow despaired and chose death.

Susan Pepper is no longer alive, at least not in this earthly dimension. It's hard to accept that truth — and to believe she is alive in my heart — so I pray for both acceptance and faith. I also pray for her, pray that in some way she finds peace, perhaps rebirth. I reach out through these prayerful words to salute Susan's strong spirit and her struggle.

Here at my desk, I imagine the lake waters spread before me, lapping at my very keyboard as I review this promise to myself and this awareness of Susan's influence. I ask the herons for help as I write, ask the spirit of the herons, ask all the winged beings who manifest the Divine Spirit to be with me, with each of us.

I loved my friend.
He went away from me.
There's nothing more to say.
The poem ends,
Soft as it began —
I loved my friend.

Poem BY LANGSTON HUGHES

. . . .

August 1997

Today I had a long run around my Britannia conservation area for the first time in a long time, glad that it's cool enough, but sad, too. How strange to run without my little dog Jessie! I am happy I've now found her a new home, yet hurting because it was too sudden for a real goodbye. I wonder if she has made the transition to her new life with her adopter better than I have so far?

On my return swing, hands empty of dog leash, but crammed with early windfall apples, there was a standing heron in Mud Lake! And yesterday evening, biking along the sunset-painted river to the west, I saw another one, far off in black silhouette. Yesterday morning in fact, I saw my first great bird since before I went to camp, so I am beginning to feel more heron-satisfied.

I truly communed with that morning heron who was fishing in Turtle Bay yesterday. It wasn't a regular heron site, though a place I hoped to see one, and I was sitting on the rock overlook, crying my eyes out. He seemed a small grey-ish heron, more than a great blue, but perhaps he was simply an immature bird; and he was undisturbed by me, as intent on feeding himself as I was on watching him.

Before walking to the overlook yesterday, I had gone out on my roller blades and fallen down twice, injuring my wrist. That very soreness seemed to trigger lots of general feelings of pain, perhaps occasioned by taking Jessie off to stay with her new owner. I don't know for sure.

In any case, I bawled and bawled, watching my heron of the day while he watched the water for fish or frogs. He barely moved, except to spear a watery meal every so often, and he seemed unconcerned with me some 20 yards away, even though I found my sore body didn't sit down slowly or gracefully as I intended it to, but rather with a thump that might have frightened him off.

I am aware of loss on so many levels: now of Jessie our former family dog, who needed to be adopted so I could be free to travel. Symbolically, I need to not have anyone else to look after — not even a dog — but only myself. Then I continue to feel the loss through suicide of Susan, my dear companion on the road of women, marriage and self-hood. She lived way up the Ottawa from me, so I didn't see enough of her, but I miss her enormously anyhow. She took her life in a tributary of this very river I love…did she fear she couldn't become the woman she longed to be? How I protest against losing her!

Yes, and I am aware anew of the loss of David, dead now for more than two years. He has been fresh in my mind and heart after attending a folk festival last weekend that we used to go to together. Afterwards I drove our daughter home for a visit. She misses David being here in Britannia much more acutely than I do, because I have lived with his absence in this place. So we both have found our memories to be hard emotional territory just now.

I feel a further sore place about Robert, who has decided to pull back from our intimate relationship. My long trip to England really underlined a growing emotional distance between us; we haven't met since I came home. He has sent no mail recently, no phone greeting for me on my return from camp; now I have posted him a perhaps problematic note saying how much I have missed him. . . All the goodbyes to each of them — our little dog; stalwart, seeking Susan; my suddenly-dead husband; my former lover — goodbyes I long to have spoken in person, all contribute to a huge aching place. And yesterday it just plain hurt, period.

After a long tearful time of perching on the rocks, my handkerchief completely sodden, I finally trudged off home, leaving the heron to his hunting vigil. Despite feeling so miserable, I was immensely thankful to have had the chance to sit with that sense of bird connection, reaffirming to myself that I, like the heron, need to alternate periods of being purposeful and moving ahead, with times of stillness.

And this morning on my run-with-apples, after I spotted the heron standing out in the midst of the swamp grasses on the north side of the lake, I tried to get closer to her, walking out to the end of a spit of land where the beavers have chewed down most of the trees. However, I had too little camouflage, and the heron flew up with a series of loud, protesting quonks and squawks. I haven't heard heron sounds all summer, and I wondered about this long "message." Perhaps I shall take it as acknowledging that I am indeed doing the right thing with Jessie, much as it hurts, and that I will come to accept the end of my closeness with Robert. My tears of yesterday have helped me towards a sense of wholeness today.

> *Our tears prepare the ground for our future growth. Without this creative moistening, we may remain barren. We must allow the bolt of pain to strike us. Remember, this is useful pain; lightning illuminates.*
>
> *The Artist's Way* BY JULIA CAMERON

An icon is something I can look through and get a wider glimpse
of God ... than I would otherwise.... It transcends our experience and
points us to something larger and greater and more wonderful.
Yes, it is an open window to God.... Perhaps we need icons because
of the very inadequacy of our ability to understand God."

Icons and Idols BY MADELEINE L'ENGLE

Over the years I have lived near herons, I have collected or been given many tangible shapes of herons — pictures, carvings, jewelry, stained glass, even dishes. And I often receive cards from different places with a heron image on them; many friends know how strongly I feel attuned to these great birds, and send me these reminders. Gradually I have spread them around the house until now I think there is something of herons in every room, and some travel with me. Each serves as a symbol and a springboard to my inner experiences of herons; each may prompt memories, but also lessons and self-questioning.

In the First Spiral I wrote of the bas relief of a flying heron that hangs on the wall of my entry-way, of how I envision its wings blessing all who come and go. But I wonder if I notice how abundantly I myself am blessed? Asking myself that is a natural part of my spiritual practice. Quakers have evolved a way of enquiring about their spiritual and everyday lives through pithy writings called "Advices and Queries." Perhaps the many visible heron images in my home are an outward way of shaping my own.

On the landing is a series of photographs of a heron wading along a waterline, seeking, spearing and swallowing his catch. Tending the plants beneath these photos, I may ask myself if I am focused on my own goals. Am I pursuing them with my own purposefulness, like the heron in search of food? What is my aim today or in the longer term?

On the bookshelf opposite my quiet morning space is a lovely MacIver watercolour of a heron about to land. Its wings suggest curving protection, even a feathery embrace. The painting is one I bought myself, to help recall the sense of being surrounded by the Divine. Can I make this truth the basis of my day?

Next to my computer, on my work table, is a tiny solid metal crane (a heron cousin), made in China or Japan, neck curled in upon itself. This image, like a large, extremely heavy pebble, is small enough to cup in my hand before I start to write. It's good to begin with that very weight bringing me fully into the present.

Another picture I look at almost daily is a large artist's photo of four immature herons crowded in their rough stick nest, apparently ready to fly out into the next stage of their lives, independence. If I pause, I find many levels of meaning in this image of pale blues and ink black, of sky and nest and bird shapes. I think of my own circle of support, contemplating the nature of my journey. Am I ready to fly on, to take another step?

A heron made of aluminum wire is poised on the windowsill behind the sink, and as I putter there, doing kitchen jobs, I often flesh out its airy shape with imagined or remembered herons standing relaxed, and attentive. For me, that is an important life-stance, being at ease in my domain, but also focused and aware.

Beside my bed are several heron feathers, half of a large blue heron egg shell, and a flat black metal standing heron about the size of a Christmas tree ornament, which hangs against the window. My eyes greet it morning and night, prompting me to ask for the same sense of inner stillness which this little heron holds. I give thanks for the gifts of the day, even as I also enumerate my struggles, and if it's heron season, the day's gifts often include sighting a flesh and feather heron.

So many gifts, so many precious symbols of Spirit, surround me. Yet there are times when they are clutter, when none of them holds meaning, when I cannot reach through to the deep inner knowledge of the Divine which I crave. Sometimes these tangible intermediaries become inadequate. Do I remember that I can centre down in Spirit wherever I am, with no external tools?

Be patient toward
    all that is unsolved in your heart.
    Try to love the questions themselves.
    Do not now seek the answers
        which cannot be given
    because you would not be able
        to live them
        And the point is
        to live everything.
    Live the questions now.
    Perhaps you will then
        gradually
        without noticing it,
    live along some distant day
        into the answers.

Excerpt from *Letters to a Young Poet* BY R.M. RILKE

Being Present

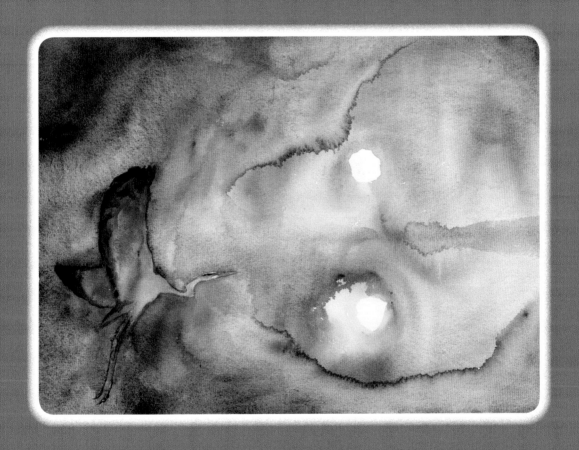

. . . .

Summer 1997

Today I stood by the shore of Mud Lake on the north side, scanning the green marshy areas and the wind-ruffled open water for any signs of herons. A big insight came to me, possibly portentous. I recognized that I often search for herons in an anxious mood, and often respond to not-seeing any herons with a sense of disappointment, of "Where ARE you? Why don't you show yourselves to me NOW?" But today that angst was tempered with the memories of being in England in the spring, of not-seeing herons most of the time there, yet being relaxed about that reality, aware somehow that on another level I was not alone, that I am always surrounded and protected, nourished and sustained by Spirit, often by a sense of being borne up by, enfolded within, great grey-blue wings.

Mostly I believe that is true, though I often have to stopper my ears to the "little brown badger voices of despair" (to use the singer Sarah Pirtle's words). My anxious looking can shift, can be replaced with an ever stronger faith that all is well, and that somewhere else a heron purposefully stalks its food, intent on its goal, as I can be.

The exciting implication of this is that I could let go of discouragement, too, as I under-stand that yet somewhere further "out there" a heron or two spreads its wings and rises. I can be confident of response, like the airborne herons mirrored in the water below. They are reflections of one another, harmonious in relationship, as we also may be. I can remem-ber that at some as-yet-unfathomed distance above me, a heron wings along its strong, sure journey, "showing" me a way forward. Sooner or later I will be able to discern my path.

Our life's companion is simply help.
Because help will come. Help does come.
Help cannot fail to come.

Life's Companion BY CHRISTINA BALDWIN

May the radiant Light and the healing Energy
of the universal Love be active in this place.
May it surround and protect,
nourish and sustain myself and each one of us.
May its peace touch our hearts,
allowing us to let go and heal ourselves.

Prayer learned from MARY ANNE CARSWELL, healer

A s I wind into the final spiral of these heron meditations, reviewing my journey so far forms a good turning point. The first significant herons presented themselves to me in 1990, and an intensity of herons had pressed upon my awareness by fall 1993. I began regular journal keeping in May 1994, and my heron reflections were a frequent part of those pages. By summer 1995 David had died, with wide-rippling after effects. That seminal shift, the herons and my growing spiritual life all contributed to major realigning and rebalancing of my personal life, home, and work.

After David's death, another completely surprising, but much more joyful, turn of events was how Robert became a dear friend and companionable lover. But by spring 1997, when I did research in Oxfordshire for 3 months, he and I were growing apart; on my return he sadly said he had decided he wanted to end our intimacy. Late that summer I also found a new home for Jessie, to free me for further travel and work in England. The next spring another friend drew close and we were intimate for almost three years. During that period I taught school and wrote for a term in England, and much of this manuscript was created. Eventually that second relationship also ended. In the spring of 2002, after a year and a half of being un-partnered and working in vain to find a publisher, as well as doing other free lance projects and school programs, I reached a cathartic moment of discouraged rebellion against how my life was unfolding — or not! Several aspects of daily life were very challenging — and then the fridge broke down, a final straw. I stormed around my kitchen, shouting at the heavens, the fates, God; everything seemed unfair!

...Remembering above all to walk gently in a world where the lights are dim and the very stars wander.

Four Stages of Greek Religion BY GILBERT MURRAY

Astonishingly, the very next day a new career arena opened in front of me, that of religious educator in the Unitarian Universalist faith community. My Quaker self is at ease there, and the work satisfying on many levels, though my Heron book project was largely on hold until Spring 2005. Next, during a year of unemployment, I made a tentative arrangement with a Canadian publisher and began to rework this manuscript. In 2006 I again took a contract as an Interim Director of Religious Education, employed in the United States for the first time since I was a young college grad. While there in Columbus, Ohio, I delved into old journals once more, re-shaping what has become the book you now hold. In August 2008, I accepted a permanent part-time position as the Director of Religious Education at the Unitarian Church of Montreal. It allows me to spend many summer weeks at home in Britannia, and so I have the balance I longed for between structured external employment and creative space.

As I read over the entire range of my heron writing pieces, I found there were a number that share a very full sense of the immediate moment, of what Eckhart Tolle calls "the power of now." Together they reflect different experiences of Spirit, herons and the natural world, and of my place in it. This spiral constitutes a single cycle through the four seasons, as well, from early summer round through June of the final entry.

... The Power of the world always works in circles, and everything tries to be round.... The sky is round, and I have heard that the earth is round like a ball, and so are all the stars. The wind, in its greatest power, whirls. Birds make their nests in circles, for theirs is the same religion as ours. Even the seasons form a great circle in their changing, and always come back again to where they were.

BLACK ELK, Oglala Sioux holy man, in *Native American Wisdom*

All the spiralling and circling around in my life often curves into glorious present-ness, being completely aware of quiet heron, wind-ruffled lake, or full heart. Mostly I am in awe and wonder during those moments; sometimes I am immensely sad or angry, yet still very rooted in that particular place and time.

These fifteen cross-sections of being present in varied ways through the yearly changing world of nature, form a whole that makes a paradoxical conclusion to my book. Of course there is an intriguing contradiction in coming to an end point made of the present! As Tolkien said so memorably, "The road goes ever on and on." May your path, and mine, continue to be blessed with insight and illumination, perhaps with a benison of herons.

EARLY SUMMER ∽ A week-long sacred dance workshop — lovely! Each morn-ing we were invited to bring any special personal things or significant symbols to put in the centre of our dancing, where our teacher spread a soft, glittery cloth and always lit a candle. My fellow dancers contributed a wide range of objects, both natural and created, and some told the group about their meaning. Glad of the invitation, on the second day I brought the big heron feather that I usually carry with my journal to the centre of our dancing circle, simply wanting to remember my heron connection, hoping it might con-tribute to our being ever more conscious of Spirit.

Later in the week I also brought in my little black metal hanging ornament of a standing heron, about four inches high, flat, but beautifully shaped in its outline; Robert gave it to me the last time we were together. Months had passed since I reluctantly agreed with his resolve to part, and I had become much stronger in myself, but I still found the issues about ending our friendship difficult and confusing. So, as a way of asking for help with them, I laid the heron image in the centre piece.

In general, dancing around that special centre was very gentle, spiritual exercise. Our teacher carefully showed the group simple steps and motions, then helped us repeat the movements until they seemed second-nature. She explained the origins of the different dances, or the meaning of the words if the music included text, and we moved — and sometimes sang — together in increasing harmony. Each dance continued for a long enough time that the repetitive simplicity became mesmerizing. Again and again, we all felt the group merge into a timeless round, at one with each other and with the spirit of all sacred dancers who had gone before us.

Personally, I loved this process of moving and melding into one graceful, centred circle. It helped when the teacher emphasized our whole body posture and suggested we be as conscious of our heads as we were of our feet. I was particularly grateful for the times when we got to dance outside on the grass and we felt at one with nature as well as with each other.

One dancing day as we circled to music near some massive pine trees, I found I was looking up, seeing sky, my shoulders back and my body supple. Suddenly I was aware of being in unity with my sense of herons as well as with the dancers, trees and sky. As I danced in a slow, stately, sacred-seeming rhythm, possibly heron-like, I was surprised to find my knotty relationship thoughts had untangled, and acceptance had replaced protest and hurt. I realized I was thankful for so much that Robert, himself a dancer, had shared with me in the past, yet I was glad in the present to be spiralling on without him.

There was no actual overflying heron in my view at that moment of intense awareness, but plenty of heron presence about. I had seen a heron the night before, in fact, winging over a nearby marshy area which gave out croaking sounds for midnight lullabies. My heron tokens were in our special dance centre piece, and I felt literally grace-full and grateful.

It is in such a state of gratitude, when we feel at one with the greater circle of life, that our anxious issues ease, that pressures and problems seem to be smoothed out, our spirits renewed. Who can prove how this happens? Was the circle dancing truly a sacred and healing process? Did my tokens actually invoke the herons and the awareness of the Divine I find through them? We only know we are marvellously connected to nature and to one another at these times, only know these are moments to rejoice.

A blue heron stalks speculatively along the edge of a pool...
To watch a wild creature move is like a visual prayer.

The Blue Jay's Dance BY LOUISE ERDRICH

... The ability to watch patiently for results.
Dignity of movement, methodical procedure
in matters. Gaining dignity and
self-confidence for facing personal problems.

CHANT: *From the stately heron I learn dignity*
Patience to wait for proper timing
By example I see the sense of methodic planning
One step at a time, personal problems are solved.

Excerpt from *Animal Magick* BY D. J. CONWAY

JULY ～ I am sitting on the rock overlook at the south end of Mud Lake, watching a heron's slow stalk out in the middle, hearing an occasional kingfisher's cry and the red winged blackbird's more constant screech in the background. As I came along the shore of Turtle Bay, at first I didn't see today's heron. Then there he was — and is still — long grey neck stretched up very thin, merging into grey sapling trunks along the shore behind him. He's moving in slow motion, easing himself towards some unseen prey.

When I did spy the heron, I stepped very carefully to a place where I could sit down, and gradually lowered my body onto this stony observation point, not wanting to scare him off. I was aware of each muscle helping, conscious of each separate stage of preparing, then sitting. It was as if I, too, were moving in slow motion, in tandem with the heron. Place the foot just so; stretch the leg over; settle into position and turn the head quite imperceptibly, breathe.

My movements, in turn, echoed a recent conversation with a healer friend. We spoke of me taking one step at a time, one breath at a time, and of how good it is to have listed my house, once David's and mine, for sale at last. Of course before listing I had to make many preparatory moves in order to even put the house on the market, such as believing the house WAS mine, and I could choose to sell it. Then there were all the practical repairs. Each of those moves was made one by one, gradually moving towards my goals. It all resonates with the Japanese saying: "Each step is the place to learn."

Clearly, I am making progress with my plans to travel and also to relocate, even if I don't know exactly where I will settle in the end. I have been to England and set up my return to teach; I have placed Jessie in a loving new home; and I have weathered the end of my intimacy with Robert. But oh, how impatient I get with myself, how I long to have resolved all the questions and problems that seem to plague my days. In contrast, I doubt that the heron ever feels so frustrated, just moves on, takes the next step in murky swamp waters, finds another frog to stalk or fish to spear.

Patience is not my strong suit, heaven knows! And needing more patience does indeed seem to be a human problem, not really an issue for the rest of creation. Perhaps the lesson we can see the birds and beasts, even the very rocks, display is that of being fully in the moment. If we are successful at being present, then we will be in less of a hurry for the next step, the next stage, next frog or swampy hunting ground. The Buddhists understand breathing into the "now" well; they counsel just sitting with a concern or simply being with the aspects of a problem, acknowledging yet simultaneously stepping back from its details.

I remember strolling one evening across the long sandy arc of Britannia beach. It was sunset, perhaps late August? There was not a human being to be seen — but there in the shallows was a slowly wading heron. Impulsively, I slowed my own pace to match his, shifting my weight forward, bending each knee joint carefully, willing myself to twin the heron's silent sequence of stalking moments.

One step at a time, I imitated my heron companion who was deliberately pacing across the orange and gold reflection-bay, seeking dinner. One step at a time, closer — then, finally, too close! The heron flew off, far upriver where I couldn't follow, and I resumed my walk. We had shared a peculiar few minutes in which, somehow, my pausing to move as he moved realigned my thoughts and increased my awareness of a still centre. Through the heron, I found more patience with myself that evening. Now, as I make each life step, may my patience grow.

Something vaster and older than what we can see and name,

the spiritual reality that is at once both within and 'beyond' the

visible world, a Presence greater even than the mountains, the sky,

the sunlight or the myriad tiny creatures parading through

the grasses at our feet.

A Faith to Call Our Own by Alex Wildwood

Mysticism for Beginners

The day was mild, the light was generous.
The German on the café terrace
held a small book on his lap.
I caught sight of the title:
Mysticism for Beginners.
Suddenly I understood that the swallows
patrolling the streets of Montepulciano
with their shrill whistles,
and the hushed talk of timid travelers
from Eastern, so-called Central Europe,
and the white herons standing — yesterday? the day before? —
like nuns in fields of rice,
and the dusk, slow and systematic,
erasing the outlines of medieval houses,
and olive trees on little hills,
abandoned to the wind and heat,
and the head of the Unknown Princess
that I saw and admired in the Louvre,
and stained-glass windows like butterfly wings
sprinkled with pollen,
and the little nightingale practicing
its speech beside the highway,
and any journey, any kind of trip,
are only mysticism for beginners,
the elementary course, prelude
to a test that's been
postponed.

BY ADAM ZAGAJEWSKI
TRANSLATED FROM POLISH BY CLARE CAVANAGH

AUGUST   ∿   A sunny, still Sunday morning. I come down to the dock at a friend's cottage, on a little lake in the Gatineau Hills. He and his partner are basking in the peace and light, and she holds a pair of binoculars. They speak of watching a magnificent heron who has now flown on; how first he stood on an opposite dock and then flew into the top of a pine tree where he poised as if a dancer, pirouetting to keep his balance, in the place of the proverbial Christmas tree angel. How next he stretched out one wing and then the other, shifting and realigning several times before flying right across the glassy lake in front of them, massive wingspread so clearly reflected they were awestruck.

I know those moments so well! Jealousy and then self-recrimination flash through my mind — how I wish I had seen that heron, but I stayed in bed too late, even though I knew the early morning was the prime time to be here at the water's edge. I remind myself as well that I needed the sleep. With a twinge of regret I remember that just yesterday I also missed a different time of heron communion:

Saturday

I ran along Mud Lake paths, carrying my binoculars, longing to see more herons than I had all week. When I got to the high rocks on the south side, I looked around the whole spread of the lake before me, checking for herons near or far. One possible tree stump many yards away seemed suspicious, so I focussed the binoculars there, and — sure enough! — there was a tall standing heron, lovely in the morning light. I saw him, but didn't stay with that point of focus, that moment of being present to the heron and the day.

Instead, I hoped almost hungrily for more, so used the glasses to scan all along the far shoreline and around the beaver lodges across the lake, spotting nothing. I also took long enough to survey the scene in this manner that I completely missed the one heron I had already seen, when he flew off. Or else he had disguised himself in the reeds and scrub trees again, because he was not to be seen when I returned my binoculars to the original place. He was still nowhere apparent to me when I then rather frantically searched the whole upper end of the lake, sure he HAD been there, just a minute before!

My Sunday dockside reverie is interrupted when we spy a family of merganser ducks swimming into view in a long line, six or seven of them, far enough away that it's hard to tell which ducks are adult and which immature. We pass the binoculars around and follow them as they swim in and out of the shadows along the other side; we discuss their colouring and head crests and wonder if there's one parent or two.

Suddenly however, the entire family disappears, and the ducks — like my Saturday heron — are nowhere to be seen! But we wait and watch, and they all appear again nearby, popping up from underwater in rapid-fire succession just as suddenly as they went under. We surmise it's a day for practicing diving and continue to watch the ducks' antics. Somehow one merganser signals all the others that it's time to submerge, and they flip down under the surface, one after another. Then a minute or two later, not too far from where they started, up they come, pop-pop-pop-pop-pop-POP! Sometimes one duck-diver-in-training seems to be too buoyant and surfaces too soon, but flips back and vanishes once more.

This synchronized duck circus carries on for ten or fifteen minutes altogether. As I enjoy it, I am again aware of the richness of being present and attentive wherever we are. I note the paradox of seeing and not-seeing, as well: of how ducks — and herons, and Spirit, too — are both with us and yet not always noticeable, some days easy to discern, popping up right in front of us, and on others, seemingly invisible.

Another day
chipped
from the stone
of time,
And in its place
the shape
of what my heart
suspects
is hidden grace.

Hidden Grace BY VICTORIA FORRESTER

To cultivate, in its root form, means to inhabit, to dwell within.
Learning how to live the dailiness of our own lives while opening
continually to the sacred seems to take practice — practice in
opening, practice in listening, practice in waiting.

The Feminine Face of God BY SHERRY RUTH ANDERSON AND PATRICIA HOPKINS

EARLY SEPTEMBER ∿ A brilliant morning today, clear and cool and still, with its hidden awareness of summer fleeting, of seasons shifting. I took my binoculars with me as I ran and was able to see four herons standing far off when I paused along the shore of Mud Lake. In their different places, each was so well camouflaged that I would not have seen them just by looking. Across the lake, the binoculars helped me spy two herons in positions which looked just like grey stumps and tall grasses. Then I discovered a third heron, so hunched beside a Canada goose sunning on the beaver lodge that at first I thought he was another goose.

Scanning southward next, I spotted the fourth heron silhouetted against the bright sun-reflecting water, atop a small new muskrat lodge. I ran on until I was quite near him. He was preening, so didn't notice my approach for some time, but eventually decided I was too close for his comfort, and lifted off, giving a quiet squawk. At first his head was so fully stretched forward that his body seemed particularly long and lean. Gradually his neck muscles settled into their usual serpentine, and he flew out of sight. Throughout that long minute of flight, low over the lake, the heron's mirrored image accompanied him on the water surface, and then it, too, disappeared.

How many more herons were somewhere out on the lake that day that I didn't see, I wonder? How true to life it is that sometimes we cannot see what is actually there, whereas other times we see clearly and even grasp how our vision is reflected back to us. This truth suggests we must not lose faith in what we have "set our sights on." So often we need help — someone else's perspective, or a different focus, like the binoculars that helped me see the herons.

This self has lately come to solitude
Who long demanded love as source and prime.
Now the wild garden and the ragged wood,
And the uncharted winter's fallow time
Become the source and the true reservoir;
Look for my love in the autumnal flower.

Excerpt from the poem *"The Image is a Garden"*
in *Letters from Maine: poems* BY MAY SARTON

MID-SEPTEMBER ∼ A plump grey squirrel has just leapt across the space between two grey metal fenceposts defining the gate where I entered the conservation area this morning. Nothing else is grey, however! It's almost the equinox, the blue air is still and clear after several days of heavy rain, and the early sunlight brightens everything it touches. Tall rowan saplings bend beneath their burdens of clustered orange berries. At a lower level, white snowberries nod between slate green leaves. Further on, deep blue black and jewel red honeysuckle berries glisten among small round lobes of leaves, similar to the snowberry bush.

At the edge of my lookout point, my favourite deciduous holly just shines, its orangey-red berries fat amid leaves of a more yellow-toned green. The short flag-staff stems of the holly bush lean out over the water: gleaming red and green sheaths reflected in burnished liquid blackness. Every view reminds me of Marge Piercy's poem *The Art of Blessing the Day*, where she glories that "... in the morning the world is peeled to shining ..." and later marvels about how "... the trees are bright as pushcart ices ..."

This sheltered bay beside the point is a typical morning sun trap, and when the weather starts to cool I often see a heron here, hunting its breakfast beside the silvery fallen tree opposite me. The tree's dead branches splay out like some huge skeletal hand, sometimes holding a kingfisher or a small greenback heron. I heard a loud, unmistakable heron quonk as I jogged towards the point, but today no herons can be seen there, only a pair of smaller birds hounding a lone crow. Out on the water, ducks and geese paddle quietly for now, though I often hear their seasonal hubbub. Far behind me a veritable murder of crows caws viciously from the tall pine grove. Heron, crows, are you announcing autumn?

Although the trees are largely still green, I run through one beautiful skiff of yellow and red-veined maple leaves, tokens of more to fall. Lately I have noted many further emblems of the season dropping towards frost and darker days. Under another maple, a random red leaf lies on a crazy quilt of tiny, dry keys — more seeds than usual, marking a golden brown circle on the wet earth. Under an oak, a black squirrel nibbles an acorn, the detritus of his meal all around him and empty acorn caps everywhere, some holding a minute drink of rain water. The squirrels have feasted in the pine trees, as well — dozens of long, tight-closed pine cones dot the ground, some gnawed upon, some less green and starting to spill their seeds. I call out my own thanks for these visual banquets I share with the created world.

At the edge of Britannia woods, the wild asters, or Michaelmas daisies, present a different palette of early autumn colours. They are appropriately named, for St. Michael's Day follows soon after the first day of fall. The tiny white ones make a cloud of flowers on their erect stalks, while the slightly larger white asters, with their yellow centres, are almost star shaped. At least two sizes of mauve ones, their centres more rusty than gold, predominate, drifting along my path and under the sumac shrubs. Every so often this spread of Michaelmas daisies is highlighted by my favourites: those painted a rich, dark lavender, occasionally more pink than purple, with larger flower heads that are more feathery-petalled. Once picked, this variety closes and withers, so I make sure I stop frequently beside them to admire their passionate purple stand. The smaller aster types keep well, however, and I often bring a handful home. They brighten my table or windowsill and, like the calling geese, will soon lure me out into the many coloured world of Piercy's "pushcart ices," of approaching autumn once again.

Something told the wild geese
  It was time to fly, —
Summer sun was on their wings,
  Winter in their cry.

Stanza from the poem *Something Told the Wild Geese* BY RACHEL FIELD

Life gets busy and thick.... Prayers come in two flavours, Help and
Thanks. I think we are at our best balance when we are saying them
together. We do, after all, need the Help. Life is very hard. Sometimes
it's so hard it's difficult not to take it personally, and that's where
Thanks comes in just right. Being grateful can smooth our way
towards some mercy for ourselves and those around us.
And to feel the beauty of the world, even amidst the hardness.

JOHN CALVI, QUAKER HEALER

FALL ≈ Out running on a windless autumn morning, I come up to my heron look-out point, and cross over a carpet of golden needles. The pine trees may not be called deciduous, but they do shed, too; suddenly the ground has a whole new silky covering. As I approach the water, pine needles slippery beneath my feet, I can hear geese honk-ing. Even though I slow down and don't burst upon the edge of the lake, the geese act alarmed to see me and set up an even louder noise. Some of them fly off in small, urgent squadrons, exciting the ducks around them into quacking, as well. Their cacophony is punctuated by a series of wing flaps as first one duck, and then another, rises up briefly, scoots farther off over the water, and, feeling safer, settles back.

Far out, beside the old beaver lodge, a heron stands quietly in early sunlight, not at all perturbed by those frightened movements. Such a clear blue October day, the air bril-liant, the lake like glass! I scan the water, dotted here and there with downy specks of white feathers floating on the shiny surface, and notice another standing heron, closer but equally undisturbed by my presence. How calm these great blue grey birds can be, how stately, almost self-possessed. How repeatedly challenging to feel as calm myself!

Then I think that the silly geese are indeed silly, their raucous noise like so much mental jabber and clutter that we must wade through to reach an inner calm, a still centre. How good to see the two standing herons, reminding me I do not need to be distracted myself, can choose not to panic or flap and flail inwardly — like the geese and ducks outwardly. I breathe in deeply, give thanks and run on.

[We reach] a new cycle of maturity where we are consciously connected to our hearts, our bodies, our deepest values, and the people we love. Our meandering paths into this new home are various.... For each of us, there is a unique journey....
We know that our journey to our old, new home is cyclical, that we shall never move in once and for all, and that we are well-accompanied by other women and by ourselves.

From the essay *"Women's Lives, Women's Stories"* BY JILL MELLICK in *Coming Home to Myself,* co-authored with MARION WOODMAN

Walker, it is your footsteps
that are the road, no more;
Walker, there is no road.
The road is made by walking.
Walking makes the road,
and on looking back
the path is seen that never
again will be the track.
Walker, there is no road,
merely wakes of boats
in the sea.

"Caminante" (Walker) in *Border of a Dream: selected Poems*
by Antonio Machado, translated by Willis Barnstone

OCTOBER ⫸ Three autumns after David's death, I was inwardly ready to move house. The time had come to live in a smaller place that was newly my own, and to sort, throw away and reorganize. However, I wanted to stay near the river and in the same Mud Lake neighbourhood (with its herons), and so I bought nearby, delighted by the opportunity.

When I took possession of my new little home, two weeks before closing the sale of the old, the first thing I planned was to hang up the small bas-relief sculpture of a heron that had blessed my previous front hall. I hammered in the new hook and rejoiced that this precious heron now spread its wings over the next stage of my life. How important it is to perform these symbolic acts! So there my heron hung, in my new entry way, serenely flying above the plaster dust, wood chips and gallons of paint.

The last day of moving out of the old home I had shared with David and our children finally came, though I was far from the end of the process of moving into my new house. There had been too many days of hard, physical work, and there was still too much to do, last minute vacuuming, the fridge to empty, and a final fire to light in the library fireplace I loved. I hurried upstairs and down, still carrying, stowing, cleaning — and watching the clock. I was determined to have some time for a quiet, prayerful leave-taking while a slowly accumulated pile of significant items burned in the old grate.

The pile-to-burn had begun when I started to pack up the library, but realized I didn't know what to do with the snake skins that I had laid across the fronts of various rows of books over the previous years. Some were still whole, but many were naturally disintegrating with age. Although each snake skin had signified the changes I myself was making, now perhaps the cast-off skins had served their purpose.

However, it wasn't until I decided to put some beautiful but dusty dried flowers into the grate that I thought of making a farewell fire from many other things I would be casting off — and to add the snake skins! And so it happened that an intriguing mix of old memorabilia, crowned with my autumnal door wreath, flamed up that afternoon, blazing merrily as I tossed on my final papery offerings. The snake skins had been signs of transformation for me, and now, as I neared the end of one major transition, those skins themselves transformed to smoke and ash.

Five o'clock approached, and there were still jobs to be done. Angrily, I acknowledged there would be no time to rest. Nonetheless, I said my prayers several times over as I dashed in and out of the now-empty library. Tears of both fury and farewell streaked my face, but they were also tears of release and of thankfulness for the new home awaiting me. The fire burned down, the snake skins were consumed, and I locked the door to the old house one last time. A small plaster heron awaited me inside my new front door.

> *Gratitude, which, like hope, is a force powerful enough*
> *to penetrate even the deep pit of depression.*

She goes on to discuss the Lord's prayer and the quotidian reality of asking for

> *our daily bread; we need to keep praying for this food,*
> *acknowledging our needs as daily, because in the act of asking,*
> *the prayer awakens in us the trust that God will provide.*

The Quotidian Mysteries BY KATHLEEN NORRIS

Prayer is about repetition. But then life is about repetition. Rivers are about repetition. sunrise and sunset are repetition. Breathing is repetition. I mean life itself is repetition. And that prayer should be repetition — how could it be otherwise?

Quote from Meinrad Craighead, in *The Feminine Face of God*
BY SHERRY RUTH ANDERSON AND PATRICIA HOPKINS

NOVEMBER ⌁ Running at noontime, on a day which began with a pink sunrise, clouded over to grey, and is now brilliantly blue. The last few yellow leaves are tossing on the maple trees, and Mud Lake is slightly ruffled. The breeze from the southeast has pushed all the flotsam and jetsam of the lake's surface up towards the north end, making a veritable scum out of hundreds of tiny feathers left by all the seasonal flocks of ducks and geese. Fringing the lake, this covering looks almost as white as ice. But we haven't had such cold weather as yet, though there are several new muskrat lodges to be seen today, and of course those feathers themselves have been shed by all the autumn migratory birds. Winter won't be far behind their stopovers! In the meantime, I can just make out two herons, one stalking a meal, the other hunched in the sun — how well they blend into the dry stalks and reeds, the sun-bleached logs and stripy stumps of this swamp. And how subtly busy all the wetland life is here — besides flotillas of waterfowl quietly feeding, I hear a kingfisher scolding, out over the water, and an insistent woodpecker drilling a tree along the water's edge.

I run on, pausing on a path through some scarlet sumac, where the red leaves are getting brown-edged. The rustier red seed heads point up at the blue sky, and then I see a chickadee land on a bush close to me. I hold up my hand towards him, calling softly, "Chicka-dee-dee-dee." Winter must be near, because he soon stops pecking at his fuzzy conical seed head of that moment, and flits closer, curious to see what food I am extending to him. I only have a few of last winter's sunflower seeds, but they tempt him to inspect my offering. Wings fast-fluttering, he hovers, swoops away, and darts back, condescending to sample one, two, then three seeds. The first two he rejects, perhaps feeling some tiny lack of weight that tells him the seed inside the hull is too dried-out, but the third he carries off triumphantly. I feel my own sense of victory, having felt the thin clutch of his bird feet on my outstretched fingers, having seen his shiny black-seed eyes eyeing me in the bright sunlight.

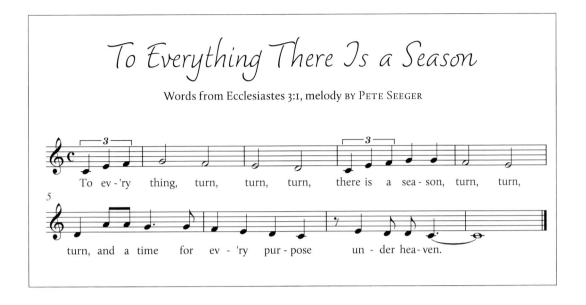

To Everything There Is a Season

Words from Ecclesiastes 3:1, melody BY PETE SEEGER

To ev-'ry thing, turn, turn, turn, there is a sea-son, turn, turn,

turn, and a time for ev-'ry pur-pose un-der hea-ven.

All these small natural riches! I am so grateful for the companionship of big and small birds, for the satisfaction of autumn coverings of coloured leaves and downy white feathers. As I step over the two sunflower seeds now fallen on my path, heading home to work with a fresh sense of focus, I realize anew how grounding I find these daily outdoor encounters.

... The circles of the seasons

within the circles of the years ...

And then we turn aside, alone,

out of the sunlight gone,

into the darker circles of return.

Excerpt from the poem *"Song"* in
The Collected Poems of Wendell Berry BY WENDELL BERRY

LATE NOVEMBER ~ Tired, tawny grass ripples across the field at the entrance to the conservation area, as I set off on my morning jog. Small grey-brown spears of wild veronica and flat-headed, lifeless yarrow flowers, both dried out and long gone to seed, present variations on the pervasive brownness extending around me on the ground. At my own head level, the rusty sumac seed heads are turning black. I run towards the woods through this landscape that lies and waits for winter. The grey underbrush grows thicker, the dun colours multiply, and then I am surprised! Right beside me on an inner stem of a honeysuckle bush, I spot a single tiny clump of shrivelled pink blossom. Did it bloom after our long dry fall, mistaking rain for spring? The petals are so pretty, yet ringed with brown where frost has touched their bravery.

Nearly the end of the month, and the weather's still relatively mild, though today there's a thin skiff of ice over the sheltered coves of Mud Lake. Overall, I decide it's a brown day: the sky is overcast, and the lake is looking muddy, after a recent torrent. The shrubs and trees surrounding the brackish water of Turtle Bay all stand naked, trunks and branches making bare lines of brown tones, sepia and grey-black. Rushes and swamp grasses fringe the wetlands with tan stalks. Weaving around the lake, where the fallen leaves haven't covered them, the encircling dirt paths reveal dark, rich earth, frosted here and there with ice crystals, but not yet frozen into the hard pale brown that truly cold weather creates. The dead leaves themselves are a palette of browns, some rotting into wet soil already, some layered in same coloured piles, compacting or disintegrating underfoot. Still other leaves spread a loose dry blanket over the forest floor, their flat shapes sprinkled with sharp, golden-brown pine needles.

Automatically, I scan the lake for herons, though I know they have gone south. Better to try and tune in to this end-of-autumn stage of nature's cycle, knowing the year will circle round, and trusting I will see my herons in abundance again when the days lengthen and they return.

For now, the fading season has other treasures, and as I savour the brownness of this morning, my eyes are drawn to a smudge of bright red. Right at the edge of the water, roots always damp, a clump of deciduous holly bushes hold up their candelabra of grey twigs and fat scarlet berries. Even without a background of snow for contrast, the leafless holly is glorious! By January, the birds will have eaten most of this brilliance, and the deep cold will have shrunk and blackened any berries that remain. Still, the holly berries are scheduled to gladden the face of winter, and they have a better chance of survival than the mistaken, valiant honeysuckle blossom.

Carefully, I pick my way over fallen logs and around boggy areas until I am surrounded by glowing holly, then judiciously clip off a few red sprays to take back and place where they will brighten up my home. Here, they punctuate the woods and waterscape on this brown day, and I understand anew the richness of the turning year.

In the Bleak Midwinter

From the poem/Christmas hymn by Christina Rossetti
Melody by Gustav Holst

In the bleak mid win - ter, Fros - ty wind made moan,

Earth stood hard as i - ron, Wa ter like a stone....

It's no accident that we all lie nestled together in the curves of the universe. We are tugged by the forces of celestial tides. Time folds in on itself and outward again in gladness as we spin around, each of us an utter miracle in a sea of tiny white stars.

Jamien E. Morehouse quotation found in Farnsworth Art Museum, Rockland, Maine

JUST BEFORE CHRISTMAS ⌇ A gift of a sharp, bright day! The sun, though near its weakest point, is brilliant this cold morning, and although there is no snow to glisten and reflect the sunlight, every low-lying object, leaf, stone or stick, is lined with thick, sparkling hoar frost. The lake is entirely frozen over, too, and all across its black glassy surface the frost has formed miraculous little clusters of stars on the ice.

Yesterday I discovered the ice was strong enough to walk on, and today I have brought my skates. At one of my favourite openings, where the path comes down to the big smooth log on the edge of the lake, I carefully straddle its frosty bulk — I feel almost wicked to mar the crystal frost patterns there, a finer, more transient surface than bark. Warily, I step onto the ice — but it's solid and sound — and sit down on a seat-size round rock to wrestle with socks and skates and laces. Even more cautiously I push off, first one blade cutting into the pristine black ice, and then the other. I stick close to the shore, but the ice is quite safe — and magnificent! Slowly I build up speed and confidence and skate through spread after spread of the miraculous ice stars, noticing cloudy bubbles frozen deep below me, crossing pressure cracks that look like hard grey ribbons.

It always amazes me to be on top of the water I so often only look at from the shorelines! How delicious to shoot along the ice so effortlessly, feeling free and unlimited. In no time I have skated half way round the periphery of the lake! Now where? Into the swamp end where thin saplings grow up through the shallow water-now-ice, and there's a natural obstacle course to try out? I skate in between and around stumps, trunks and small muskrat mounds, delightedly exploring. This is an area where there are also plenty of dead trees that the herons roost on in their season, but where it's very hard to walk or canoe to watch them. Now I can be a winter visitor to their summer territory.

Skating out again onto a wide expanse of ice, where next? Shall I go nearer to the middle of the lake and carefully check on the beaver lodges there? The busy beavers have still kept some open water around their constructions, so I must beware of that, but I am glad to be able to examine their habitat more closely than the shore view permits. How I love to sample the space where herons often stalk or wait! Perhaps I am partaking in the freedom of wild things as I skate so joyfully. Certainly the saying "free as a bird" makes complete sense!

Everywhere I skate, frozen things sparkle and shine. Back along the shoreline, but on the far side of Mud Lake, where I seldom venture, I stop to admire frost asterisks all along a piece of dark wood held in the ice. The sun catches the frosty edges of dry grass leaves, makes each line of icy embroidery twinkle. My spirit feels as bright and special as the day. O thanks, Great Spirit, for all this cold creation, for all that I seem to see as new!

Now, in the evening, I sit by the window, look out at the mountain, close my eyes, and hundreds of wings come toward me. So many wings inside me, a heart full of wings, arms, toes, brain, tongue, all wings. And a huge motion goes through me, and we travel together.

A Walk Between Heaven and Earth by Burghild Nina Holzer

We fit within and belong to the universe ... [not] separate from and superior to all of the other forms and life-forms — animals, vegetables and minerals — that in concert make up the universal symphony.... We are stanzas within a universal song.

Hymns to an Unknown God BY SAM KEEN

DEEP WINTER ~ Out early in the cold air, snow crisp underneath, and the sunlight brilliant. I decide to ski right across Mud Lake, passing the newer beaver lodge, inspecting a muskrat home en route, all the way to the swampy-now-icy east end and back. As my skis rhythmically skim the surface, crunching more than cutting through the snow, I realize that I seem to be on a kind of heron patrol, visiting all the sites where I so often see herons standing in the warm weather, when I am usually confined to the shore. Near the old beaver lodge I even find some of the silvered curving stumps which in some lights deceive me into thinking they themselves are herons.

Winter seems so absolute in mid-February that it's hard to recall all the growing season colours of green leaves, orange jewelweed and purple loosestrife stalks — all I can see of them today are dry brown stems and branches, sharp outlines against the hard whiteness of the lake. And yet, just as I know the herons will return, so will summer. I notice with joy how the sun has melted a little hollow around each stump and stick protruding through the ice. Wherever there is a darker surface to soak up the sunlight, the warmth is slowly winning. The days are lengthening, and soon this frozen white expanse will crack and melt. Then there will be feathered wings beating across Mud Lake, making different sounds than my swift sliding skis. In the meantime, this "swish, swish" calms me, unites me with subzero nature.

So, too, the spiritual life, with its mystical inner heartbeat, is always beating around me. Sometimes I sense a divine universal pulse as I watch the seasons shift or listen to the wild birds or the rushing river rapids. Sometimes I need silence to remind myself. Sometimes it comes upon me *in medias res*, in the middle of the river of life — or of a frozen lake.

Once in Quaker Meeting for Worship, back in a different February, well before this skiing experience, I had a similar sense of a mysterious, silent rhythm. It was so profound, and I felt so centred, that I discovered I was composing a poem in my head as I sat motionless. The lines slowly formed themselves as I breathed; nothing else seemed to fill my consciousness but these words, which I wrote down immediately after the end of the Meeting, not waiting to shake hands or do any of the customary greeting:

Into the silence we come
spirits seeking, mind and bodies
willing to be still, be slow,
praying to the Source:
above, around, below.
Sometimes we are distracted,
our thoughts go —
elsewhere.... So
gently return.
The deepest silence
is Divine, I know.
Out of this silence
blessings flow.

Meeting for Worship, February 9, 1992

LANDSCAPE

Isn't it plain the sheets of moss, except that
they have no tongues, could lecture
all day if they wanted about

spiritual patience? Isn't it clear
the black oaks along the path are standing
as though they were the most fragile of flowers?

Every morning I walk like this around
the pond, thinking: if the doors of my heart
ever close, I am as good as dead.

Every morning, so far, I'm alive. And now
the crows break off from the rest of the darkness
and burst up into the sky—as though

all night they had thought of what they would like
their lives to be, and imagined
their strong, thick wings.

"Landscape" in *Dream Work* BY MARY OLIVER

EARLY MARCH ~ After a few days performing in Toronto, I travelled home to Ottawa. Southern Ontario, in the warmer climate zone of the Lake , had had a week long thaw, so that there was very little snow cover left anywhere. Only dirty, icy piles left by the snowplows told a wintry story, but the mild weather receded as I drove north east.

The sky was cloudy that day, and snow flurries periodically filled the air. Where the snow settled on the bare ground, it made a thin layer of white almost-mistiness. Grassy hillsides looked as if they had been sprinkled with flour. In the woods, in between the dark tree trunks, the effect of light snow on tan leaf cover was dappled, different from the solid blanket of white striped with black — tree lines — that had extended everywhere as I left home the previous week. Fall-plowed fields were stippled with miniature white snow caps and tiny light valleys emphasizing brown ridges of earth. Now the grey rock faces, instead of being covered with ice or white drifts, were also etched in white lines where snow flakes filled crevices and cracks. I savoured that drive, with all its views of the season — of course, nothing except the pine trees was green. However, in many open areas, the reddish stems on the low scrub bushes of osier dogwood were starting to glow: sap was rising in more than the maple trees! I got home to find that Ottawa had had a warm spell, too, and wrote in my journal:

...The foot or more of snow I left behind has now dwindled to very little: bare brown patches of lawn and garden soil show through all around the house. Happily, last night's snowfall has dusted the grey icy remains of snow, hard trodden along the paths, or heaped up around the edges of streets and driveways, with a lovely fresh whiteness. I set out to explore my old familiar world once again on an early morning walk, optimistically wearing running shoes. In the conservation area, dry grasses dominate the field, with thin stretches of snow and ice lying low between pale stalks and old seed heads. Puddles along the paths are frozen over, but their ice cracks when I test the surface, and here and there brown muddy water oozes out from underneath.

Similarly, the ice is soft around the edges of Mud Lake, and I suspect there will be no more skiing across it this year! Somehow the thaw has emphasized lots of footprints: I see rabbit, fox, dog and human tracks in sharp relief. Someone's long past snowshoe marks, marching over the lake, have dwindled into a raised trail where each frozen footprint looks a like squat white toadstool. The animals' paw prints are fresh, so they are still clearly unafraid to traverse the ice. I, however, only step carefully alongside it, marvelling at the signs of life everywhere in this late winter landscape.

Squirrels scurry away from me, chasing each other round tree trunks, and woodpeckers hammer nearby. Chickadees and nuthatches are busy pecking at bark and branch in the undergrowth that surrounds me. Crows call and caw in the distance, and many three-toed crow's claw marks are branded into the icy trail I follow — in several places, there must have been crow congregations! Then a line of tiny paw prints crosses my path through the woods: is this a small creature newly emerged from hibernation? High up in my favourite grandfather oak tree, I spy the old porcupine sleeping in a spiny ball. Inwardly, I salute them all and head home, deeply refreshed.

After a trip away, immersing myself in the details of the natural universe around me helps me come home to my particular physical place within the Infinite.

> *The marshes of the wildlife refuge…. I have come here before,*
>
> *to this place of the birds. This year I came to find refuge myself,*
>
> *from heaviness and grief…. At one time I looked through the*
>
> *binoculars and had an eagle, a hawk and a great blue heron*
>
> *all in my picture at the same time, coming toward me.*
>
> *… Mount Shasta in snow, in full volcanic majesty,*
>
> *shimmering in the background. I love this earth.*
>
> *A Walk Between Heaven and Earth* BY BURGHILD NINA HOLZER

SPRING ∼ April has come and gone, and this early May morning finds me out jogging. The sun is brilliant, and the air warm enough to run without a sweatshirt, though it still has a cold edge. There is "a certain sharpness in the morning air" as poet Mary Oliver puts it so eloquently. I have been away for a few days, so there are lots of changes to explore in the conservation area. Spring in eastern Ontario is advancing slowly but steadily, and the herons are back, though I didn't spy any today. I saw my first one, just for a fleeting moment as it flew low over the trees near the river rapids, late last month on Good Friday, and the next day there were two more herons out in Mud Lake. I felt a surge of Easter joy-in-resurrection when I saw they had returned! After the sometimes interminable winter, the harsh enduring cold, how delighted we are to emerge and find fresh life! For me, such a seasonal emotion parallels Mary Oliver's conclusion in her poem, "that love itself, without its pain, would be no more than a shruggable comfort."

Strangely, although Easter moves on the calendar, it is often when I see my first herons of the season. At least once before this I saw them anew on Good Friday, which

fell on an equally grey day as this year. However, I remember that years-ago-April as
a much snowier month, recall rubber-boot-wading through both icy melt pools and
deep piles of old snow, back in among the aged willow trees, and then looking upwards
through black tree branches to see a heron pump its wings above us. I can still feel
myself standing, awestruck, as I followed its flight. That was early on in my heron years,
when I had less knowledge of their ways, less accumulated communion with the herons
to reflect upon.

But this day, though the trees are largely still bare, there are other springtime
reflections, other creatures to watch in sunny silence. Two mallard duck males, their
vibrant green heads glinting, swim away in watchful alarm as I pass the north end of the
lake. Just beyond them a huge black crow rises from the water's edge into fat-bud maple
branches, its wings rustling. A downy woodpecker pecks at the old seed heads of a slim
sumach, voicing a small peek! peek! at me. Then I notice that the honeysuckle shrubs
are sporting small tufts of green leaves already. Farther on I spy a couple of wood ducks,

I rose in the hour before dawn. I would go out into the

rich darkness, into a thrilling invisibility, and, intensifying it,

swim in the blackness of the lake, in the path the moonlight made.

I would walk east to the marshy ground where herons sat folded

in the tall dead elms, and watch the first streaks of green swell

with light and shrink and deepen into dawn....

The Names of Things BY SUSAN BRIND-MORROW

the elegant curve of their heads emphasized by the thin white feathered calligraphy lines around their eyes. Shyer than the mallards, they fly up hastily, landing again mid-lake, the shape of their heads arching so beautifully against the sky-reflecting water.

Running back towards the woods, along the shore road, my eye is caught by something shiny and black at the base of some tall dried bullrushes. Just as this round shape shifts, I see several more gleaming black domes — oh, I exult, the turtles have come up out of the mud to sun themselves! Spring really has arrived! However, the big turtle propped against the bullrushes, arranged at the most favourable angle to the sun, is frightened by me and slips into the water; two others plop-plop after him as I run on.

Their appearance spurs me to jog around the arm of the lake at the other end, which I call Turtle Bay, where there are dozens of yellow-bellied Blanding's turtles (and a few snapping turtles, too) in season. Sure enough, the warm sun has lured them all out onto every dead log and half-sunken tree trunk in the bay. Everywhere I look there are rows of shiny black-button turtle shells, and on one especially long old trunk I count at least twenty five! Sometimes a disturbance will cause the turtles to dive back into their muddy lake waters with a series of splashes, one after another, like some animate, rounded, game of dominoes falling in sequence. This time they're far enough away that none are scared off, and every log keeps its turtle buttons.

I linger in the same spring sunlight those little turtles enjoy, soaking up my own sense of well-being. Like them, I am ready for the season's turning, but not impatient. May I remember Mary Oliver affirming "... that even the purest light, lacking the robe of darkness, would be without expression." Let each day bring more buds unfurling, more birds returning, more moments of oneness in the light.

{Jogging}, pulled forward by the golden light of day's end, shining off the trees and road surface. I'd speed into the orange orb of the sun as if it would swallow me in its glow. My body and soul breathed light, swallowing it in great gulps of joy.

Proverbs of Ashes BY RITA NAKASHIMA BROCK

In this ordered and creative chaos that I will always be fashioning into the narrative of my life, I am sustained by an abiding trust that, as Isak Dinesen said, "God made man because He loved stories." Without my autobiography and yours, the story of the universe would be forever incomplete.

Hymns to an Unknown God BY SAM KEEN

JUNE ∿ I am lying on a towel on the floor in a body awareness class, along with about half a dozen other women, and the leader is talking us through a series of moves. It is early on a Saturday morning, warm enough to be wearing just a t-shirt and shorts. My t-shirt happens to have a glorious heron image on it; it was a birthday gift from a friend who knew how pleased I would be with it.

The floor is hard beneath my back, yet my body is fairly relaxed and my mind feels present in the moment, aware of each small movement we are tasked with. "Notice your shoulder blades," I hear the leader say, "Check whether they are both equally in contact with the floor. Are they different? Feel how your spine touches the floor, feel each vertebra." When she finishes leading us through our trunks and limbs, she suggests we concentrate on our heads. "Turn your head to the left side and try not to be tense in your neck. Now let the plane of your chin be parallel to the top of your shoulder. With your eyes closed, in this position imagine that your nose is pointing to the left ... and breathe in deeply."

Suddenly I am filled with an unexpected merriment, an inner chuckling contentment! As I focus my awareness on my nose, I realize my own nose is lined up with the sharp pointing beak of the large heron head-and-shoulders portrait on the t-shirt which covers my breast. My t-shirt heron is drawn in a side view, with its S-curve neck, head plumes and strong beak all turned to the left, as my head now is. It is totally surprising, yet seems so fitting, and funny, too, to consider that I myself am long necked and also have a straight pointed nose.

I often think of myself as like a heron, but this moment carries more meaning than that simple recognition. Here, aware of the warm summer air around me and the position of each bone and fingertip resting on the rough towel surface beneath me, I have a profound sense of once again lining myself up to the Divine. It's as if the heron image has literally pointed the way to the Great Alignment. My nose is parallel to the painted heron's, my heart is open to the universe, and quiet happiness suffuses me, top of head to tip of toe.

The wide wings flap but once to lift him up.
A single ripple starts from where he stood.

Excerpt from *"The Heron"* in *Collected Poems of Theodore Roethke*
BY THEODORE ROETHKE

I celebrate the rich and varied materials I have drawn on over many years that have now been woven into *The Heron Spirals: A Commonplace Book*. Many people have freely granted me permission to quote their work, for which I am deeply grateful.

All sources are referenced in the text where they appear. Authors or publishers who have requested a specific annotation are listed in these credits below. In addition to those works credited here alphabetically, fuller information on certain details or persons cited is given in the Notes, listed by page number.

All reasonable efforts have been made to seek permission for the materials quoted, and any errors are my own. If you have corrections or concerns, please contact me at carolinebp@sympatico.ca; if you have material to share, I would be delighted to have you add it to my website page for the book: www.carolinebalderstonparry.com/site/the-heron-spirals

CREDITS

TED ANDREWS, *Animal Speak: The Spiritual and Magical Powers of Creatures Great and Small* © 2002 Llewellyn Worldwide, Ltd. 2143 Wooddale Drive, Woodbury, MN 55125. All rights reserved, used by permission.

CHRISTINA BALDWIN, *Life's Companion, Journal Writing as a Spiritual Quest,* and *Storycatcher, Making Sense of our Lives through the Power and Practice of Story.* Reprinted with the author's blessing. www.peerspirit.com

JOAN GOULD, *Spirals, A Woman's Journey through Family Life*, Random House, New York 1988. Used with permission of the author.

SUSAN GRIFFIN, *Women and Nature: the Roaring Inside Her,* Copyright © 1978 by Susan Griffin. Reprinted with permission of Sierra Club Books.

KATHLEEN NORRIS, *The Quotidian Mysteries: Laundry, Liturgy and "Women's Work,"* Paulist Press, New York/Mahwah, N. J. 1998. Used with permission of Paulist Press. www.paulistpress.com

MARY OLIVER, "Landscape" from *Dream Work*, copyright © 1986 by Mary Oliver. Used by permission of Grove/Atlantic, Inc. Any third party use of this material, outside of this publication, is prohibited.

ALICE OSWALD, excerpt from "Pruning in Frost" from *Spacecraft Voyage 1: New and Selected Poems.* Copyright © 1996, 2007 by Alice Oswald. Reprinted with the permission of The Permissions Company, Inc. on behalf of Graywolf Press, Minneapolis, Minnesota, www.graywolfpress.org

MAY SARTON, excerpt from "The Image Is A Garden" Copyright © 1984 by May Sarton, from COLLECTED POEMS 1930-1993, by May Sarton. Used by permission of W. W. Norton & Company, Inc.

BROTHER DAVID STEINDL-RAST, *Gratefullness, the Heart of Prayer: An Approach to The Life in Fullness,* Paulist Press, 1984. Used with permission of Paulist Press. www.paulistpress.com

NOTES

p. 7   The Rev. Dr. Nita Penfold, the Director of the Unitarian Universalist teaching approach called Spirit Play (www.spirtplay.net) coined the phrase "the power of love and mystery that some call God."

p. 14   Mary Jo Leddy notes: "I tend to imagine the Holy Spirit as a Great Blue Heron" in *Radical Gratitude*, Orbis Books, 2002.

p. 19   The blessing from the Latin came to me through Grace Wallis, a now deceased friend in Witney, Oxfordshire.

p. 25   My Westtown School Grade 11 English teacher, Chuck Kruger, was an early support for my poetry, and he also edited a near-the-end draft of this manuscript. Chuck now lives, writes and tells stories in Cape Clear, County Cork. www.chuckkruger.net

p. 26   The 17th century Quaker who spoke of feeling "wound into Largeness" was Richard Hubberthorne, quoted by Ernest Taylor in *Richard Hubberthorne: Soldier and Preacher* (died 1653), Friends Ancient and Modern, #16; Friends Tract Association, New York, 1911. I found the quote in Pendle Hill Pamphlet #340 "A Song of Death, Our Spiritual Birth: A Quaker Way of Dying."

p. 28   In the *Folklife Center News,* Spring 1999, article "Dance Music of Oklahoma's Yuchi Tribe," author Jason Baird Jackson notes:
"The Yuchi (Euchee) Native people once lived throughout the region now known as the Southeastern United States. Dance songs were and are an important part of traditional Yuchi religious ritual. The group of songs which used to accompany their summer 'feather dances' are believed to have been provided to the Yuchi people in ancient times by the white crane. These lines from a traditional origin story are given here with line breaks representing the spoken rhythm of traditional Yuchi oratory."

p. 44–5   The Cable TV documentary referred to is titled "The Search for the Sacred—Quakers." It can be seen at www.youtube.com/watch?v=LaSsPBNGVpU

p. 47   My search for the author of the song "Spirit of the Wind" was assisted by Brooke Medicine Eagle, www.MedicineEagle.com, who has recorded a full version on her CD "Gift of Song."

p. 50   Rabbi Steven Greenberg was interviewed as part of the additional materials with the film "Trembling Before G-d;" 2001, DVD 2003.

pp. 52 and 58   Christina MacEwan is a sculptor as well as a poet, with a superb website: www.christinamacewensculpture.ca

pp. 62 and 95   The authors of *Out of The Skin* used several classic children's books or stories as the basis of their work, including Barbara Cooney's *Miss Rumphius* (Viking, 1982), long a favourite of my own. Before her death she gave me permission to write a song I have called "The Ballad of Miss Rumphius," but not to record it. I will be glad to share the words and tune informally.

p. 91   The classic book *When Bad things Happen to Good People* was written by Harold Kushner, a Conservative rabbi, in 1978.

p. 105   Michael Leunig is referred to as "an Australian national living treasure" on his Facebook page. The quote is from his little book of illustrated prayer-poems titled *The Prayer Tree*, published in 1991.

p. 114   The last line of this small song's text, new to me, was contributed by Laurie Doerfler, a friend in Columbus, Ohio, after the first edition was printed. Clearly the folk process is still alive!

p. 141   Mary Anne Carswell's website is www.editors.ca/profile/724/mary-anne-carswell

p. 154   John Calvi's website is www.johncalvi.com

p. 166   Mary Oliver has also written a number of lovely poems about herons. I had to choose just one poem to include, however, and this one fit this Spiral elegantly.

RODERICK MACIVER, ARTIST

Roderick MacIver is a nature artist concentrating mostly on water media (watercolors, acrylic ink). For twenty years he was Director of the nonprofit art publisher Heron Dance, and his published works include *Thoreau and the Art of Life* and *The Heron Dance Book of Love and Gratitude*. His latest book is *Wild Waters and the Tao*. He divides his time between Vermont and The Split Rock Wildway, a nature preserve in the Adirondacks of New York state. www.roderick-maciver-arts.com

NOTE ON THE TYPE:

This book is set in Calluna and Calluna Sans — contemporary typefaces designed by Jos Buivenga.
The script typeface is Dolce, designed by Elena Albertoni.